8 Habits of
Effective Small Group Leaders

"Here's the bottom line: If you practice Dave Earley's 8 habits as a small group leader, you will successfully lead and multiply your group. Pastor — Getting your group leaders practicing these skills will mean success for your church at reaching lost people while discipling and pastoring your members through your small group structure. What Dave Earley does do is break it down into bite-sized pieces that any sincere small group leader can master. Sign me up for the first 100 copies that come off the presses. I want every one of my group leaders to read this book again and again."

JAY FIREBAUGH
Senior Pastor, Clearpoint Church in Houston, TX

"Outstanding! Practical and proven steps, workable tools, and inspiring stories make this a MUST READ book for anyone who has anything to do with small groups. Dave Earley has done an excellent job of capturing the essence of what it takes to be an effective small group leader!"

KAREN HURSTON
Author and Director, Hurston Ministries

"Do not ignore the powerful instructions in this book. Practicing these habits will ignite your small group and revolutionize your ministry. Each chapter contains a treasure chest of practical insights that you can pull out and use today."

DR. RALPH W. NEIGHBOUR, JR.
Author and Founder, TOUCH® Outreach Ministries

"Earley's book is necessary reading for group leaders who desire to grow spiritually and who need a plan to see growth in the groups they lead. This easy to read book is practical, profound, and highly relevant. Many readers who have seen their small group ministries grow will recognize some of the 8 Habits. Earley puts all 8 habits together in a coherent, interesting, and highly readable package."

MIKEL NEUMANN
Author of Home Groups for Urban Cultures

8 HABITS

OF EFFECTIVE SMALL GROUP LEADERS

8 HABITS

OF EFFECTIVE SMALL GROUP LEADERS

Transforming Your Ministry
Outside the Meeting

BY DAVE EARLEY

Cell Group Resources™, a division of TOUCH® Outreach Ministries
Houston, Texas, U.S.A.

Published by Cell Group Resources™
P.O. Box 7847
Houston, Texas, 77240, U.S.A.
(713) 884-8893 • Fax (713) 896-1874

Cover design by Mark Nebauer Designs
Text design by Rick Chandler
Editing by Scott Boren

Library of Congress Cataloging-in-Publication Data

Earley, Dave, 1959-
    The 8 habits of effective small group leaders / Dave Earley.
    p. cm.
    ISBN 1-880828-34-0 (pbk.)
    1. Leadership—Religious aspects—Christianity.   2. Church group
work.   3. Small groups.   I. Title: Eight habits of effective small
group leaders.   II. Title.
    BV4597.53.L43 E36 2001
    253'.7—dc21
                                            2001004621
                                                  CIP

Cell Group Resources™ is a book publishing division
of TOUCH® Outreach Ministries, a resource and consulting ministry
for churches with a vision for cell-based or holistic small group-based
local church structure.

Find us on the World Wide Web at
http://www.touchusa.org

ACKNOWLEDGMENTS

Together everyone accomplishes more. This book is the product of the contributions of many others. I want to thank my wife, Cathy for her wonderful encouragement, editing, support, and understanding. I appreciate my editor, Scott Boren, who not only gives great advice, but also is as excited about this book as I am. Joel Comiskey's research and books have taken my understanding of small group ministry to a new level. Thanks to Larry Stockstill for being a great example of a senior pastor of a growing cell-based church. I need to thank the many small groups and small group leaders I have experimented on over the years. I must thank Lee Simmons who encouraged me to lead my first small group at CHS and Roy Rhoades for making me do it. Thanks to Ed Dodson, who going against his better judgment hired me to oversee small groups at Liberty. Thanks to Mom and Dad for their prayers. And I certainly need to thank the entire staff at New Life for their encouragement, advice, examples, and constructive criticism. Special thanks to Susan Chittum who is the glue and to the Big Three, Steve Benninger, Rod Dempsey, and Brian Robertson because I would be worthless without them.

CONTENTS

Part One: THE EIGHT HABITS OF EFFECTIVE GROUP LEADERS

Part Two: THE EIGHT HABITS OF EFFECTIVE CHURCHES

FOREWORD

I first met Dave Earley twenty years ago when he was an undergraduate student at Liberty University with a vision of planting a church in Greater Columbus, Ohio. That original vision has never wavered, and now it has been fulfilled. Today, there is a wonderful church in Columbus, Ohio; however, the vision does not stop there. The original vision of one church has become a 20/20 vision of planting twenty more churches in the area in the next twenty years. I believe he will do it; let me tell you why.

When Dave Earley graduated from Liberty University in 1985, I publicly predicted Dave would plant and grow the largest church in America of any of our graduates. Some might have thought that our graduates who were powerful pulpiteers or great fund-raisers would build greater churches. But I stood by my prediction because Dave has discipline in his personal life, in his handling of finances, and in his commitment to reach the "Boomer" population (when Dave went to Columbus, he was able to reach and win young families).

Today the church has had two thousand in attendance on special days and a weekly offering of over $40,000.00. Read this book carefully to learn how your church can do the same thing.

First, Dave believes in team ministry, he and four other graduates from Liberty University and Liberty Baptist Theological Seminary have worked hard to fulfill their initial vision of planting a vibrant church in Greater Columbus. After sixteen years the team is still together — that's unparalleled in Christian work. Even though Chris Brown, the original youth pastor, has gone to start his own work in Columbus, he is still a part of the original team and a part of their 20/20 vision. A high school student that was reached by Chris Brown — Matthew Chittum — has graduated from Liberty University and is now planting a church in the Greater Columbus area. Dave's team has a good start on their vision, two churches of their 20/20 vision have already been planted.

The small group concept that Dave Earley describes in this book is not a theoretical one. He began the first small group of the church in his home when he arrived in 1985. He has done everything he asks you to do in small group ministry.

The church has grown through small groups. Some people came to the church through the small groups, others came to the main service, but they have been "bonded" to the church through involvement in small groups.

If you do not read anything else in this book make sure you read and apply chapter eight, "Be Committed To Personal Growth." Dave tells you how he has personally grown in Christ and spells out a personal growth plan that you can follow. Outstanding!

The last thing I want to say about this book is that it is written well. I should have expected it knowing that Dave does everything with commitment. You will learn a lot without wasting time reading non-essentials. You will get more out of the book because it is done well . . . to the point . . . and in an interesting manner.

Enjoy learning *The 8 Habits of Effective Small Group Leaders*.

Sincerely yours in Christ,
Elmer L. Towns, Dean
School of Religion
Liberty University
Lynchburg, Virginia

INTRODUCTION

Why do some small groups grow and multiply while others do not? Is there some activity or set of activities a small group leader can do to increase the probability of the group growing and multiplying? If so, are these activities beyond the reach of the average small group leader? Will it take years of training to master them? Or, is there a set of activities that are attainable and realistic that any small group leader who wants to grow and multiply can put into his or her weekly schedule?

I believe I have an answer to these questions. I have had the privilege of leading small groups and coaching small group leaders for twenty-five years. It began when, as a 16-year old, several friends and I started lunchtime Bible studies at our high school. They "accidentally" grew and multiplied. In college, I started a discipleship group that spread over the campus. During my summers, I started groups in little towns in England and in high rises in New York City. After I graduated, I started groups in rural Virginia. Then, I was hired to train, write curriculum for, and oversee 300 small group leaders at a large Christian university. Later, I started a group in my basement that grew into a church with over one hundred groups.

Some of these various groups grew and multiplied; others did not. Through the years, I have noticed the long-range effectiveness of leaders revolves around simple habits that those leaders practice outside of the group meeting.

Many leaders sincerely want to grow and multiply their groups, but they are not sure how. They work on finding better icebreakers or asking better discussion questions. While these are valuable things, the real key to growing and multiplying a small group lies in the practice of eight personal habits.

Several years ago, I wanted to show the leaders I was coaching exactly what it would take for them to be highly effective. By studying small group ministry and thinking through my own experience I came up with eight regular practices that seemed to make the difference between effectiveness and ineffectiveness. I put them into a concise list of eight habits that would enhance the effectiveness of a small group leader.

I began asking the leaders I coached to adopt these habits and build them into their weekly schedules. Without exception, those who used these habits became highly effective leaders who grew and multiplied their groups. Those who did not, did not. What was especially interesting was that gifts, personality, and experience were not as important as commitment to the eight habits. Leaders who did not have the gift of teaching or had not been Christians for a long time but who followed the eight habits became effective. Leaders who tended to be quiet or had never led before but who practiced the habits were growing and multiplying their group. The eight habits made the difference.

After teaching these habits for several years, I have come to several conclusions:

1. The eight habits work. Following the eight habits of an effective small group leader makes all the difference between mediocrity and greatness, between stagnation and multiplication. Following them will produce growth, develop future leaders, and add to what God wants to do.

2. The eight habits are universal. They apply to all cultures and all types of groups. They are foundational principles that work for any type of group and any type of leader. They are usable with any group of people whatever their age, race, gender, or socioeconomic status. They can be lived in the inner city or on the farm. They work for those on a college campus, those in a foreign nation, and those in the suburbs of the U.S.

Although some see a distinction between "small groups" and "cell groups," in this book the terms are treated interchangeably. This is because the eight habits are universal and apply to both.

3. The eight habits have broad application. One beautiful fact is that they are essentially the same habits that produce effectiveness for coaches of small group leaders, zone directors, and small group pastors. Once a leader incorporates them, he or she has the foundation for moving up the levels of small group leadership.

4. These habits are easy to understand and remember. I have seen small group leaders' eyes light up as their mentors explain the eight habits to them. Leaders nod their head and say, "Yes. I see. That's simple enough. It's just common sense."

5. The best quality of these habits is that they are doable. Any leader can put them into practice, if he invests the time. When small group leaders hear the habits explained, they nod, saying things like, "This is just what I have been looking for. Now I have a clear course to follow. I can do this."

6. The eight habits are realistic. Most leaders can fit them into their busy

schedules. It does not take a spiritual giant or someone with unlimited time to do them. These eight habits are attainable goals for all small group leaders.

7. The eight habits are motivating. Upon learning them, leaders burn with the passion to put them into practice. The eight habits are challenging, but not overwhelming.

The eight habits can take a small group leader, and those under him or her, to a new level. Whether an apprentice leader, a novice small group leader, a seasoned leader, a coach of small group leaders, a director of a district of groups, or a pastor of a large small group ministry, the eight habits will work. These habits lead to fruitfulness and multiplication. The eight habits will help leaders, and those under them, experience greater fulfillment in ministry.

The Eight Habits of Effective Small Group Leaders

1. Dream of leading a healthy, growing, multiplying group.
2. Pray for group members daily.
3. Invite new people to visit the group weekly.
4. Contact group members regularly.
5. Prepare for the group meeting.
6. Mentor an apprentice leader.
7. Plan group fellowship activities.
8. Be committed to personal growth.

THE EIGHT HABITS OF EFFECTIVE GROUP LEADERS

Part One

DREAM:

Dream of Leading a Healthy, Growing, Multiplying Group

Two couples received the same small group leader training. Chris and Susan began a new group with the dream of ministering to single adults in a healthy, growing, multiplying group. Mark and Kathy took over an existing group because one of their pastors asked them to, but they did not have their own dream for the group. For the first six months, both couples worked hard at inviting and contacting people but both groups stayed small.

Mark and Kathy got discouraged. They soon lost what little dream they had for the group and began to go through the motions of group leadership. They stopped praying for their people or contacting them regularly. They quit inviting new people. They did not take much time to prepare for the group. They stopped having fellowship activities. The dream was gone. As a result, their small group kept shrinking. Within a year it died, and they left the church.

Chris and Susan did not lose sight of their dream. They worked hard to apply other habits that would help their dream. Eventually their efforts started to pay off. Within a year, their group had taken off. It continued to grow and eventually it multiplied. The dream made the difference. The first habit of the highly effective small group leader is to dream of leading a healthy, growing, multiplying group.

> **The first habit of the highly effective small group leader:**
>
> **Dream of leading a healthy, growing, multiplying group.**

The Value of Having a Dream

Having a Dream Increases Potential

Most small groups and small group leaders are sleeping giants. Satan wants to keep them that way, so he constantly whispers lies to small group leaders about what they can't do. Satan is defeated when small group leaders get a dream of what they and their group can become. Their ability to make a difference for God's kingdom immediately rises.

Effective small groups have staggering potential. Our church began as a single small group meeting in my basement; it now has over one hundred small groups. The Methodist church traces its beginning to a small group that met at Oxford University, and today it has over 11 million members.

If a small group leader multiplies his group into just one other multiplying group every year for ten years, the results are incredible. After the first year, 1 has become 2. At the end of the second year, 2 has become 4. After the third year, 4 has become 8. Then 8 groups become 16, 16 become 32 groups, and 32 become 64 groups after the sixth year! Then if multiplication continues annually, 64 groups give birth to 128, 128 groups to 256, 256 groups to 512, and 512 groups become 1028 groups by the end of the tenth year. Over 1,000 groups in ten years! Such is the possible result of a single small group!

Effective small groups are the untapped potential of the local church. Not only can they multiply to reach large numbers of people, but they can be spiritual hospitals for the hurting and hothouses for spiritual growth. They can be the breeding ground for leaders and the launching pad for spiritual warfare. They can give people a feeling of belonging. Effective small groups can create evangelism teams. Yet this potential often goes unrealized without a dream.

Someone observed that the potential of a man is measured by the goals he pursues. Few people realize even a small fraction of their potential. Having a dream helps a small group leader begin to realize his awesome potential to make a difference for God.

Dream the dream of leading a healthy, growing, multiplying group. Dream of leading your group to multiply every year. Believe that God can use your small group to make a big difference.

Having a Dream Aids Accomplishment

I started a group several years ago. I never had a dream for that group. I started it because a man asked me to, and I felt obligated. It was simply a weekly meeting of a few men to study the Bible. The group never jelled and never grew; within a year, it died a quiet death.

On the other hand, I started a group last year with the dream of growing and multiplying it within a year. I practiced the habits of highly effective group leaders. In nine months, it grew and multiplied into four groups. The difference was having a dream; it motivated me.

Dreams aid accomplishment. There are many good things in life I never would have accomplished without a dream. Had I not first dreamed about it, I would have never led someone to Christ, read through the Bible, or planted a church. And I have never successfully grown and multiplied a group that I did not have a dream of growing and multiplying.

Having a Dream Focuses Direction and Channels Energy

Through the years, my boys have played a variety of sports. I learned to coach my children by observation and by trial and error. I have been their coach in a variety of sports, but not soccer. I never had the privilege of playing soccer and still struggle to understand the fine points of the game.

When my youngest son Luke was five years old, he was on a team coached by a man who understood soccer, but not coaching or children. The team was struggling terribly in the early part of the season.

One blistering day the team had practice on an open field. For the first 15 minutes, the kids just ran around and either misbehaved or complained about the heat. The coach got a call on his cell phone and had to leave. He looked around and, seeing me standing on the sideline, asked me to take over while he was gone.

The first thing I did was put a couple of traffic cones up to serve as goals. I then put the kids on teams and told them to try to work the ball toward the goals and to see if they could kick it into the goal and score. Half an hour later, the coach returned; he was stunned to find the kids working together, working hard, and having fun. He grabbed my arm and said, "How did you do this?"

"Goals," I said. "The kids just needed some goals."

Without goals we lose focus, fail to channel our energy, and are hindered by obstacles. Goals are dreams in increments. Highly effective small group leaders have a big dream broken down into specific, simple, attainable, and challenging goals. They set goals for such habits as praying (chapter two), inviting new people (chapter three), contacting members (chapter four), mentoring apprentices (chapter six), having fellowship activities (chapter seven), and growing personally (chapter eight). Then, they plan these habits into their weekly schedule (chapter nine). They also set goals for attendance and multiplication. Finally, they channel their efforts into reaching those goals and fulfilling their dream.

Having a Dream Increases the Value of the Group

A dream puts everything into perspective. Even tasks that are difficult, mundane, or unrewarding take on added value when we know they will ultimately contribute to the fulfillment of a dream.

Effective small group leaders don't just "lead a group." They raise up leaders to reach the world. They help the body of Christ minister to its members. They create a spiritual family and build a spiritual army. When small group leaders understand this dream, they immediately raise the value of their groups in the eyes of each member.

When the value of a group is raised through a dream, the leader is changed. The dream of group health motivates the leader to pray for her members and to prepare for group meetings. The dream of group growth inspires the leader to contact and invite people. The dream of multiplication sparks the leader to take the time to mentor upcoming future leaders.

When a leader shares the dream of health, growth, and multiplication, that dream changes the people. Once they buy into the dream, members will pray for the group. They will not want to miss a meeting. They will invite others. They will more easily care for, share with, and appreciate one another.

Having a Dream Positively Predicts the Future

A study of Harvard graduates revealed the power of written dreams in positively predicting the future. Forty years after graduation, researchers found that 5 percent of the class had accomplished more than the other 95 percent combined. This 5 percent had one thing in common: they wrote out their goals while in college. The other 95 percent also had something in common. They had not written out their goals.

In his research of the world's most effective small group-based churches and leaders, Joel Comiskey also found the power of dreams to predict the future. He writes,

> *Cell leaders who know their goal — when their groups will give birth — consistently multiply their groups more often than leaders who don't know. In fact, if a cell leader fails to set goals that the cell members can clearly remember, he has about a 50-50 chance of multiplying his cell. But if the leader sets goals, the chance of multiplying increases to three out of four.*[1]

Having a Dream Motivates Leaders to Keep Going

Leading a small group has its share of setbacks. People promise to come and then do not show up. An apprentice is transferred by his employer a few weeks before he assumes leadership of the group, setting back multiplication. People don't always get along. Dreams help a leader keep going in spite of the obstacles.

Obstacles can be described as "those frightful things you see when you take your eyes off your goal." Having a dream will keep a leader going in spite of obstacles and setbacks. Highly effective small group leaders know that having long-range goals keep them from being frustrated by short-term failures. Every leader and every group suffers setbacks. But highly effective leaders don't quit. They stay motivated. Their dreams keep them going.

Three Dreams of a Highly Effective Small Group

Highly effective small groups reach for three attainable dreams. The highly effective small group leader dreams of seeing her group grow in quality, increase in numbers, and multiply into multiplying groups. Each part is very important.

Group Health

A highly effective group is a healthy group. There are various elements of group health. The most obvious is the noticeable presence of God. People come not because their friends are there, but because God is there.

Many good things happen when God is there. People really care for each other. Guests are invited and welcomed. The Lord is fervently worshipped. People hunger for the Word of God and how to apply it to their lives. Members feel loved and accepted. Relationships are developed. Spiritual growth occurs and lives are changed.

> Highly effective small group leaders dream of seeing their group:
>
> Grow in health, increase in numbers, and multiply into multiplying groups.

Health Barriers:

- *Pride.* James 4:6 says that God "opposes" or literally "stiff-arms" the proud. Isaiah 57:17 says that God dwells with "the contrite and lowly in spirit." Do not allow pride to keep God away. Cultivate the presence of God by cultivating a humble spirit of gratitude and dependence upon Him.

- *Sin.* Psalm 66:18 tells us that sin keeps God from hearing us. Sin in the lives of the members or leaders will limit the presence of God in the group. Leaders need to welcome the presence of God by confessing sin and teaching group members to do the same.
- *Unresolved conflict.* Matthew 5:23-24 tells us that unresolved conflicts hinder our ability to approach God. Help people resolve conflict biblically, privately, and effectively so as to not hinder the group's ability to worship God.

Sincere praise and worship welcomes God's presence during the group meeting. Few things can stimulate group health like genuine prayer and fasting by the leader prior to the group meeting. (See chapter two, Pray.)

Group Growth in Numbers

The highly effective group increases in numbers. The law of nature is that living, healthy cells grow. Growing groups see attendance grow as group members remain faithful, unconnected Christians join the group, and the lost are won to Christ.

Growth Barriers:

- *Limited physical space.* My favorite professor, Elmer Towns, often said, "You can not put 17 ounces of cola into a 16 ounce bottle." He meant that physical space limits group growth and size. Some groups cross this barrier by meeting at a larger place. Many have the children meet in a separate room. Others divide the men from the women at least part of the time. And of course, growing groups eventually solve the space problem by multiplying into two groups.
- *Lack of spiritual life.* People do not usually hang out at morgues. People are drawn to life, not death. A group that is not experiencing spiritual life and health will not grow. Members will not invite guests. Visitors will not come back. People will drop out.
- *Lack of intentional outreach.* New people do not "just show up." They are invited. Growing groups take time weekly to pray for not-yet-in-the group people. They strategize the best means to reach them. They plan activities to draw and connect them with the group and encourage one another to invite them. (See chapter three, Invite.)
- *Failure to maintain contact with the members.* Group members will miss group meetings. People get sick. They get tied up late at work. They go out of town for a week or two. They stay home to help the kids with a science project. And if no one contacts them in between small group meetings, one week's absence turns into two. Two weeks turn into three and soon they are no longer a part of the group.

Growing groups regularly contact all members and always make the effort to contact absentees. (See chapter four, Contact.)

- *No social activities to bond the group and attract new people.* "All work and no play make Jack a dull boy." And all meetings and no social activities can make the group a dull place. Humans are social creatures and enjoy occasional social outlets. (See chapter seven, Fellowship.)
- *Failure of the leader to share responsibilities with apprentices.* The solo leader will reach a limit of what he can do. When his limit is reached, the group stops growing, unless he shares responsibilities with others. (See chapter six, Mentor.)

Group Multiplication.

The highly effective group leader will help develop new leaders and new groups. Healthy cells will not only grow; they will multiply.

Multiplication Barriers:

- *Failure to have and mentor apprentices.* New groups must have new leaders. Groups fail to multiply when they have no apprentices to become leaders of the new groups. Try not to start any new groups unless they are already pregnant. A pregnant group is one with an apprentice or apprentices already in place being prepared to eventually lead new groups.

   But it is not enough to have an apprentice. The group leader needs to mentor the apprentice to develop as a group leader. (See chapter six, Mentor.)

- *Failure to plan to multiply.* Some groups have apprentices but never seem to have enough momentum to multiply. Many groups have found that the momentum needed to multiply comes after a plan to multiply is in place. This simple plan primarily involves the date and method of multiplication.

The Small Group Leader's Personal Dream of Group Health, Growth, and Multiplication

Pray right now about your dream as a small group leader.

Write out your dream in your own words and/or use the statements below.

- I have the dream of leading a healthy, growing, multiplying small group.
- I will learn the habits needed to make this dream come true.
- By God's grace, I will live the habits needed to make this dream come true.

_____

_____

Sign and date this commitment.

Name: _____

Date: _____

Read the statement of your dream regularly and make it an ongoing focus for prayer, learning, and effort.

If you are already leading a small group, dream of the best strategy and date for multiplying your group. Discuss it with your overseer. Write it below.

_____

Plan various ways that you can continually share the dream of being a healthy, growing, multiplying group with your group.

_____

Plan various ways to regularly share the date and method for multiplying with your group members.

_____

PRAY:

Pray for Group Members Daily

Many years ago, evangelist S. D. Gordon said, "The greatest thing anyone can do for God and man is to pray." After 25 years of leading small groups and coaching small group leaders, I have come to one clear conviction: prayer is the most important activity of the small group leader. If a small group leader could do only one thing to make the group more effective, that one thing would be to pray.

Prayer is a fascinating tool for the person with a heart to minister to others. It is one of the simplest things we can do. All we need to do is sit down and lift someone up to the attention of God. Yet most of us will admit that it is one of the hardest things to do for others. We get busy. We get distracted. We get discouraged, and we just don't pray enough.

Highly effective small group leaders view prayer as a non-negotiable aid in their ministry to others. They use it often and well. They build it into their daily schedules and make it a high priority. They don't just pray a little; they pray a lot.

> The second habit
> of the highly effective
> small group leader:
>
> *Pray for group members daily.*

Reasons Effective Leaders Pray for Members Daily

Prayer is the most important task of a leader

You cannot find an effective spiritual leader in the Bible, or in history, who was not a person of prayer. This is the reality today as well. A survey of small group leaders revealed an interesting correlation between time spent in prayer and small group multiplication. It revealed that leaders who spent 90 minutes or more in daily devotions multiplied their groups twice as often as those who spent less than half an hour.[1] Taking the time to pray makes a difference!

Prayer is the most important task as a small group leader. Success here will make success in the other habits much easier. Failure here will make success in the other habits nearly impossible.

Prayer saves time

The biggest obstacle to prayer is that we are overwhelmed by our daily tasks. We never seem to have enough time. One of the biggest excuses made for not praying enough is being too busy. Such a statement reveals a misunderstanding about the nature of prayer. We fail to understand that prayer actually saves time and effort.

Prayer allows God to do things in short periods of time that we could not accomplish without Him in months or even years of work. How often have we taught, encouraged, counseled, and rebuked people with little or no result? How often have we shared our faith with seemingly little or no breakthrough in another person's defenses? But when God moves, He helps people make changes in seconds, where we could not get them to do it in years. Prayer is a powerful time saver. Once we understand this we must learn to say, "I am too busy not to pray."

Martin Luther, the very busy founder of the Lutheran Church, understood the power of prayer to save time and effort. He once told his barber, "I generally pray two hours a day, except on very busy days. On those days I pray three."

Prayer is omnipresent and omnipotent

Prayer touches omnipresence. It invites God to work in people's lives even when the group is not meeting. You can't meet with all of your small group members 24 hours a day, but God can. You can't go with all of your small group members to their homes or with them to work, but God can. You can't be at two or more places at once, but God can.

Prayer also touches omnipotence. It brings God into the situation; nothing is too hard for God (Jeremiah 32:17). He does great things as a result of prayer.

I have the delight of church members coming up to me and saying, "Pastor Dave. I have been praying and you will never believe what happened!" I always smile and say, "Tell me, I believe it."

At our church, we recently completed eight days of prayer and fasting. During that week, our members saw God do many God-sized things. These included the spiritual rebirth of a 99 year old relative, the breaking of a decade-old addiction to cigarettes, a $1000 need met by an unexpected gift in the mail, and several people sharing about the offer of new jobs with significant pay increases. Prayer is a very powerful activity.

Prayer makes everything better

No one ever comes to the end of their life saying, "I prayed too much." But many come to the end of their lives saying, "I prayed too little." No small group leader has ever looked back and said, "I think I spent too much time praying for our group this week." But too many look back and say, "I think I spent too little time praying for our group."

Prayer has a way of making all things better. Prayer makes you a more loving and spiritually sensitive leader. It causes the small group meeting to spring to life. It makes preparation for the small group meeting go quickly and smoothly.

Prayer energizes small group members in between sessions. It makes inviting new people more effective. It makes finding and mentoring an apprentice easier. It adds fun to small group socials. It draws your small group members together. Prayer is always a plus.

Prayer gives needed insight

True prayer not only speaks, but also listens. Prayer connects us with God, and God knows everything. When we listen in prayer, God gives us insight into important matters. Suddenly, we have new understanding of our members' needs, strengths, struggles, and potentials. We can recognize the right person to recruit as an apprentice. Prayer is a necessary privilege and responsibility.

The priests of the Old Testament, including Samuel, were responsible to stand before God on behalf of the people. Failing to pray for the people was considered a sin (1 Samuel 12:23). Most pastors have too many people to pray for individually. But if each small group leader would pray for his or her people, the task would be done in a very effective way.

If leaders do not pray for their members daily, who will? If people do not need anything else from other Christians, they do need prayer. All of us need prayer all of the time. We need prayer for our spiritual, emotional, physical, and financial needs. We need prayer for our marriages and our children. We need prayer about decisions. We need prayer about our jobs. Pray for your people and teach them to pray for you, and everyone will benefit.

We ask all of our leaders to make a commitment to set the P.A.C.E. for the people under them. P.A.C.E. stands for Pray daily, be Available in time of need, Contact regularly, and be an Example of a progressing Christian. Notice that Pray comes first.

Prayer is our greatest spiritual weapon

No one has led a small group for long without running into serious spiritual conflict. Two of the things Satan fears most are prayer and multiplication; both are in the DNA of effective small group life. Small groups develop leaders and equip ministers to take ground from Satan.

A leader must pray to keep from being defeated by Satan's persistent attacks on himself and on his small group. To fail to pray is to fail altogether. Satan will not let us simply plunder his kingdom. He will not just allow us to grow and multiply, evangelize and equip. He will fight us every inch of the way.

We must not only pray to keep from losing ground, but also pray in order to take ground. On our own, we can not overpower the enemy, but when we pray we walk in power. We can fight him successfully from our knees. We can march forward on our knees. Only one weapon will hold him off and push him back. It is the weapon of prayer. This is why we must pray without ceasing.

God blesses us when we pray for others

Job suffered crushing trials. He lost his children, his business, his servants, his crops and livestock, and his health. His body was covered with oozing boils. His friends accused him of bringing it all on himself by disobedience. His wife encouraged him to curse God and die.

Suddenly, Job's health was restored and he had twice as much as he had before. He had a new brood of children, and his friends honored him. He had twice as many flocks and servants. What caused such a miraculous change in fortune? Job prayed for his friends (Job 42:10).

God blesses us when we pray for others. When we pray for their health, he blesses ours. When we pray for their children, he blesses ours. When we pray for their marriage, he blesses ours. When we pray for their finances, he blesses ours. God blessed Job when he prayed for his friends. God blesses us when we pray for others.

Tips for Highly Effective Prayer

Have a set time and amount of time for prayer

Those who don't have a set time for prayer rarely take the time to pray. Great people of prayer speak of their appointments with God. Most agree that the when of the time is not as important as having a time. Set aside a time when you will meet God daily. Make it your unbreakable appointment with God.

It is good to set a goal for the amount of time you will spend in prayer. A beginner may start with 10 to 15 minutes and grow from there. An hour in prayer would be a great goal to reach. If that seems like a lot, realize that the more we pray, the more God will work. The small group leaders making the greatest impact are the leaders spending time in prayer.

Have a usual place for prayer

Our ability to focus and concentrate in prayer is enhanced by having a regular, private place for payer. Jesus spoke of this private place in Matthew 6:5-7. He promised that the God who sees in secret will reward us openly by answering our prayers. Find a place where you can privately and passionately pour your heart out to God.

When my children were little, we lived in a very small house. I found that the best place for me to pray was the sidewalk of my neighborhood as I walked for exercise every morning. Now, I pray in my office or as I walk on a nearby track in the mornings. I often go to a park and sit on a picnic table and pray. Where you pray is not important, but find a place to pray.

Have a plan for prayer

Many great prayer warriors speak of using the disciple's prayer of Matthew 6:9-13 as a plan for prayer. They use it as an outline including worship (vs. 9), petition (vv. 10-11), and confession (vs. 12). They cover these areas once or even several times when they pray.

Others use the acronym ACTS (Adoration, Confession, Thanksgiving, and Supplication) as their prayer plan. But the specifics of the plan do not matter as much as having a plan.

Have a place for recording requests and answers

The weakest ink is better than the strongest memory. We do not want to forget someone's requests or needs, but often we do. It is valuable to have a list or, even better, a small notebook in which to record prayer requests. Then you have it right in front of you as you pray. It also becomes a testimony of the many prayers God has answered. When I get discouraged I often get one of my past prayer notebooks and look at all the answered prayers.

Ask God to direct you to appropriate Scriptures

Sometimes we are not sure what we should be praying into a person's life. When in doubt, Scripture is the best thing we can pray. Paul left some great examples of prayers he prayed for those under his care (Ephesians 1:17-19; 3:16-19; Philippians 1:9-11; Colossians 1:9-12; 1 Thessalonians 1:2-3). I have special verses God has directed me to pray regularly for my children, my wife, and my key leaders.

Season your intercession with thanksgiving for each member

It is easy to get frustrated with the people we are called to lead. They sometimes act like sheep, wandering off in all the wrong directions. The apostle Paul seemed to keep amazingly free from the frustrations of spiritual shepherding. I think one of the reasons for this was that he persistently thanked God for them. Notice that Paul consistently begins his letters and prayers with words of gratitude to God for his people. (Ephesians 1:16; Philippians 1:3-4; Colossians 1:3-4; 1 Thessalonians 1:2).

Mix fasting with prayer for greater effectiveness

Many prayer warriors have discovered a "secret" of prayer: fasting. Fasting is voluntary abstinence. It generally involves abstaining from food for a period of time in order to focus on God and give ourselves more wholly to prayer. Typically fasting lasts for one complete 24-hour period, usually from sundown to sundown. The early church fasted two days every week, Wednesday and Friday. Pharisees fasted Tuesday and Thursday. Other biblical fasts ranged from three to forty days. Both individual and corporate fasts are seen in the Scriptures.

I generally fast for about 20 hours before my small group meets on Wednesday evening. This means that I eat dinner on Tuesday evening and then don't eat solid food until late afternoon on Wednesday. When I fast, the group seems to flow better, and I seem to do a more effective job leading the group.

Pray through all possible elements of the small group meeting prior to the meeting time

It is better to pray before trouble comes. Job prayed and sacrificed for his children daily in case they sinned (Job 1:5). Think of all the possible elements of the small group meeting and bathe them in prayer. From the attendance to the worship, from the prayers to the discussion of the Word, cover each with prayer. This will give you peace and confidence that God will be able to do all He wants to do in your gathering.

Pray for your apprentice(s) and the future groups to grow out of your current group

We will talk more about mentoring apprentices in chapter six. The key to remember is your group cannot multiply unless you find and develop apprentices to take over future groups. Jesus told his disciples to pray for the Lord of the harvest to raise up laborers for the harvest (Matthew 9:38). Good apprentices are harvest laborers in the highest sense. They help you reap and maintain your harvest and will one day multiply it as they lead their own groups.

When leaders ask me where to go to find apprentices, my answer is always the same: "On your knees." God is the one who can send you an apprentice. God is the one who can help you find untapped potential in the people in your group. God is the one who can guide you in bringing out the best in them. You just need to ask Him.

Pray for God's grace to help you

The other eight habits are discussed in the rest of this book. For now, start with this significant practice of prayer. Pray about your prayer life. Ask God to help you build it into your schedule and your life. With prayer, all the other things you do will be better. Without it, all the other things you do won't amount to much.

Prayer is the most important habit of the highly effective small group leader. Apply this chapter by filling in the small group leader personal prayer chart.

The Small Group Leader Personal Prayer Chart

My daily prayer time _____

The amount of time is _____ minutes a day.

I have a place to record answers and requests:

    Yes: _____   No: _____

My place for prayer is _____

My plan is _____

_____

_____

_____

_____

_____

_____

INVITE:

3

Invite New People to Visit the Group Weekly

I had seen John at church several times. He and I started our friendship during a camping trip. I knew he needed to get going spiritually, and I had been praying for him. One evening, I saw him at church after he had dropped one of his kids off at an activity. I had asked God to give me someone to invite to my men's group that week, and I felt God tugging at my heart to invite John. I wasn't sure how he would respond, but I plunged ahead.

"Hi John! How's it going?"

He looked at me and said, "Ok, I guess."

"Hey I was wondering, do you have a small group you attend regularly?" I asked.

John got an amused smile on his face and said, "Funny you should say that. I was talking with my wife at dinner and told her I needed something to get me spiritually geared up."

"Well," I smiled at him, "I have a men's group that meets on Monday evenings. Why don't you give it a try?"

"I think I will," he said.

John tried the group that Monday night. During the group, he made a tearful re-connection with God and a meaningful connection

The third habit
of the highly effective
small group leader:

*Invite new people to visit
the group weekly.*

with the men who prayed for him. He has not missed a meeting in over a year.

Highly effective small group leaders build several disciplines into their schedule. One that is often overlooked, but highly important, is the habit of inviting new people to the group.

Reasons Why Inviting is Essential

People must connect with you before they can connect with God

Modern missions leader Donald McGavern said, "Relationships are the bridges of God." People get connected with God by first making a connection with God's people.

National surveys consistently show that 80-90 percent of those who visit a church and those who come to Christ both do so at the invitation of a family member or friend.

If your group has no guests, it will experience no growth

Your group can't grow unless you have and keep guests. This may seem ridiculously obvious, but it is often forgotten. If no one new ever visits your group, your group cannot grow. Increase the number of guests and you will increase the amount of growth. Increase the rate of retention and you will increase the rate of growth. Increase both and you will multiply growth exponentially.

Why do some groups grow and others don't? Why can some leaders consistently grow their groups and others can't? The answer often lies in the issue of inviting. Those leaders and groups that consistently invite new people will grow. Those that don't, won't.

Occasionally I talk with group leaders whose groups aren't growing. They act like the new people visiting their group have fallen from outer space or dropped in off a cloud. They seem to think that having new people come is a matter of fate or a mystical work of the Spirit. Now it is true that on rare occasions the Holy Spirit will supernaturally drive someone to attend a group without being invited. But this is maybe one out of every thousand guests. The other 999 times new people visit a group, it is because they were invited.

Seeing new people visit your group is very practical. Before guests will come, they need to be invited. People don't just magically show up. Someone must take the initiative to ask them to come.

Every time I have practiced the habit of inviting someone every week, the group has grown. Every time I have not consistently invited new people to come, the group has not grown.

If you invite them, they will come

Some group leaders don't invite people "because they might not come." When people tell me this, I always ask, "If you invite them, what is the worst thing that could happen?"

They generally respond, "They might not come."

Then I reply, "If they are not coming anyway, how have you lost anything? After all, they just might come."

I like to say, "If you invite them, they just might come." In fact, it is exciting to know that if you invite them, they will come. Not all will come. Not all will come right away. But if you invite them, some will come.

According to Richard Price and Pat Springer,

Experienced group leaders . . . realize that you usually have to personally invite 25 people for 15 to say they will attend. Of those 15, usually only 8 to 10 will actually show up, and of those only five to seven will be regular attenders after a month or so.[1]

This means you can grow a new group of ten to fourteen regular members in a year by inviting one new person each week! A wise leader tries to invite at least one new person a week and encourages the members of his group to do the same.

If you will invite enough people, some will come. When I start a new group, I start by asking two to five times the number of people I expect to have at the first meeting.

Some ask, "Where do I find people to invite?" There are at least five good types of people to invite.

Types of people to invite:
- *Family.*
- *Friends.*
- *Coworkers or fellow students.*
- *Neighbors.*
- *Church contacts.* (This would include those church members who are currently unconnected to a group and new guests who visit your Sunday worship services.)

Inviting stops declining numbers

The average church in America loses 10 percent of its membership annually.[2] Likewise, your small group will lose people. Therefore, without guests, your group will not only fail to grow, it will decline.

Five ways people leave:
- *Drop out.*
- *Move to another part of the country.*
- *Move to another church in the area.*
- *Move to another group or ministry within your church.*
- *Become leaders in a new group.*

Numerical growth builds excitement and morale

People respond positively to progress and negatively to the lack of it. Groups that continually add new people have a greater level of excitement and a higher morale. Members are proud to be a part of a group that people want to visit.

Inviting builds spiritual ownership of the group

Inviting helps people take ownership. They make the change from speaking of "the group," "your group," or "their group" to "my group" once they take the step of inviting someone to the group. This is a huge element in helping them accept ownership of the group. It increases their commit-ment to the group, their level of participation in the group, and their concern about the group. The wise leader motivates his members to invite others for no other reason than helping them develop greater ownership.

Mistakes to Avoid in Inviting

Failing to saturate the situation in prayer

God knows the "what, when, where, and how" of an effective invitation. Prayer helps us cooperate with what He is doing.

Failing to keep them saying "Yes"

Once someone has said "No" to an invitation, it can be easier for him to say "No" to the next invitation. So it is valuable to get him to say "Yes" and to keep him saying "Yes." If possible, build a bridge of "Yeses" until he is a regular attendee of your group.

For example, some people invite a person to a group before the person is ready to say "Yes". But the person may be ready to say "Yes" to allowing her children to attend a children's activity at the church. A progression of "Yeses" may look like this: "Yes" to dinner at your house; "Yes" to letting you pick up her kids to attend a function at your church; "Yes" to a 4th of July fireworks party for the family at the church grounds; "Yes" to the Easter musical, a special Sunday church service like a Friend Day or Easter Sunday, or Christmas Eve.

Finally, they are ready to say "Yes" to your group. Obviously, different people and different churches have different progressions of "Yes." Pray about finding the thing someone will say "Yes" to, and start from that point.

Let me encourage you not to make the mistake of taking it personally when people you invite say "No." Too often, we get our feelings hurt and withdraw from the people we feel have rejected us. Instead, we need to keep caring for and loving them.

Giving up too soon

Too often, we invite someone once, and he says "No." So we do not invite him again. Too frequently, we invite him to come, and he says "Yes," but doesn't show. So we don't invite him again. And sometimes, we invite him to come, and he comes but doesn't come back. So we don't invite him again.

Too often, we are guilty of giving up on a person too easily. Persistence makes a difference. I find that many people who don't come at the first invitation often come after the third or fourth if I have continued to build a caring relationship.

I knew Todd for several years. He had not shown much interest in attending church. However, he had allowed his kids to attend our Vacation Bible School. Over the years, I earned his trust and planted the seed. So, I invited him to a Friend Day at church; he told me he was busy jet skiing with his family every Sunday. So I waited until the weather got too cold to jet ski and invited him again. This time he said "Yes" he would come, but he never showed up. I kept working on building our friendship. Not long after that, he told me his wife wanted a separation. This time, he asked me about coming, and he has been consistent ever since. God has wonderfully changed his life. I am glad I didn't give up.

Failing to understand the principle of "Six to Stick"

Realtors tell us that it takes about six solid contacts to fix their name in the minds of prospective clients. I have found it also takes about six contacts by a group leader to fix his group in the mind of a potential member. You want to help people think, "If or when I ever go to a group, I want to go to that group."

Some people make one attempt at getting people into their group and think their effort was a failure when those they invited don't come. Maybe it wasn't a failure; maybe it was a step in the right direction.

Failing to pray for and capitalize on opportunities

I was at a baseball game watching my fourteen-year old son play shortstop. I had planned on inviting someone to a Friend Day we were having at church that week, but I hadn't had any opportunities. I quietly asked God to give me one. There was a single mom whose son was pitching for my son's team. He had been one of my son's teammates for a few seasons, and I had taught him how to pitch. As I walked by her, I felt the prompting of God to invite her. The next thing I knew I was telling her about the Friend Day at church and asking her if she and her son would like to come. She said they lived near the church. Her son had visited some of our youth activities and liked them. So she thought maybe they would come.

At the next game, I told her more about Friend Day. She said that she had mentioned it to her son; they thought they might try it.

The next week they came. Afterward she said, "I came because of my son, but I have to admit that I absolutely loved it." They came back every week. A few weeks later her son was saved. Three months later she was saved and was not only a regular attender at our church, but also a member of my small group.

Failing to win the three victories

Probably the biggest reason why genuine attempts to invite people fail is that the inviter has failed to understand the principle of "the three victories necessary to win a soul." You must win these battles in order to win the war.

The three victories to win the war for a soul:
- *Win them to you*
- *Win them to your group or church*
- *Win them to Christ*

Inviting is not effective when we fail to win people to ourselves first. If they do not know or like you, then they will not visit your group. If we have not won them to ourselves, they feel no desire to come and will often make excuses for why they can't come.

But once we have won them to ourselves, several good things happen: we know how, what, and when to invite them. They are willing to listen to our invitations. They get to see the difference the group makes in our lives.

Then we can win them to our church or group. From that point we can win them to Christ. I find that the people with whom I win all three victories are people who will stick with God and stay with our group.

Trying to be a solo inviter

Inviting is easiest when inviting is done in concert with a team of people, a posse of prayer, and a healthy group and church. You do not have to do it all by yourself. It is especially powerful when a person already knows and likes someone else in your church or small group.

Failing to capitalize on the seasons of the soul

People have seasons of the soul when they are more open to the gospel.

Most adults come to Christ, or come back to Christ, during one of these seasons:

The seasons of the soul:
- *Death of a loved one*
- *Move to a new neighborhood, city, job, or school*
- *Divorce*
- *Marriage*
- *Family problem*
- *Major illness*
- *Birth of a child*

The wise leader is sensitive to these seasons. He lovingly uses them to increase his ministry to the person he hopes to invite.

Tammy came to a group in the early 1990's and met Christ. She was excited and so she brought some of her Catholic friends and neighbors. One was Lori. Lori came once or twice but liked her regular Catholic life. Tammy eventually joined our church and grew in Christ. On the other hand, Lori experienced divorce and then discovered she had cancer.

Through it all, Tammy and some of her other Christian friends loved Lori. Out of her despair, Lori cried out to God and met Him in a powerful way. She started coming to our church and joined the ladies group Tammy was attending. God put it all together to draw her to Him during a dark season of her soul. Now Lori is a member of our church and an apprentice in a small group!

Using inappropriate levels of pressure

I have noticed an interesting phenomenon while shopping for cars. The better the car, the less pressure from salespeople. They don't attack you when you drive onto the lot. They give you time to inspect the car for yourself. They give you time to think things over. When salespeople are confident that the car is good, worth the price, and saleable, they don't twist your arm to make a deal; they just confidently describe their product.

The wise group leader also has confidence in her group. She knows it will be a wonderful blessing to anyone who gives it a try. She doesn't twist arms; she just confidently describes her group. She speaks of answered prayers, changed lives, and warm friendships. She doesn't use inappropriate levels of pressure.

Suggestions for What to Say and When to Say It

Comments that will whet their appetite:
- We have a wonderful group.
- God is answering our prayers.
- People in our group really love each other.
- Almost everyone in our group [is single, has young children, is newly married, etc.] just like you.
- We could use [a sharp thinker, a person with a good sense of humor, another big-hearted person] like you.
- We would love to have you join us.

Statements that plant the seed:
- You will like it.
- You will fit right in.
- We will love to see you walk in the door.

Questions that drop the bait:
- Do you have a group you meet with weekly to study the Bible?
- Our group meets at such and such a place at such and such a time. Why don't you come?
- Let me personally invite you to come. We would love to have you join us. Do you think you can come?

Declarations that show the power of the group:
- We have been praying for your [grandmother, job, operation, son, etc.].
- When people visit once they almost always like it and come back.
- Once people get hooked on our group, they don't ever seem to want to leave.

Answers to their concerns:
- You don't have to know anything about the Bible to come.
- You don't have to read, pray, or sing aloud unless you want to.
- You don't have to dress up. No one else does. I usually wear jeans.
- All the kids [go to the kids club, meet in another room and have their own story, meet with us]. My kids will be there. They really love it.
- If you come and really don't like it, we won't make you come back.
- It's a singles group, but people are there to meet God, not just find dates.
- It's okay if you arrive a little late. We eat and drink coffee the first ten minutes anyway.

The Small Group Leader Personal Inviting Chart

My weekly inviting time _____

The amount of time is _____ minutes a week.

People I can invite:

- Family: _____   _____

  _____   _____

- Friends: _____   _____

  _____   _____

- Neighbors: _____   _____

  _____   _____

- Co-workers or School Friends:

  _____   _____

  _____   _____

- Members of my church who are not connected to a group:

  _____   _____

  _____   _____

- Guests to Sunday Worship services:

  _____   _____

  _____   _____

- The person I want to focus on this week is

  _____

My plan is _____

_____

_____

CONTACT:

Contact Group Members Regularly

4

When I first began to walk with God as a sixteen-year old, I quickly learned where I could get the best breakfast in town. Every Saturday, I would go to the church kitchen and enjoy a huge breakfast. A team of smiling grandmas laid out pancakes, sausages and gravy, scrambled eggs, donuts, juice, and milk for us. And it was absolutely free. All you had to do was promise to go on bus ministry the rest of the morning.

In the 1960's and 70's, the bus ministry phenomenon swept through evangelistic churches. Churches bought used buses, gave them a fresh coat of paint, and filled them up with unchurched children on Sunday mornings. The success or failure of the bus ministry revolved around the principle of contact: that is, if you continue to contact them, they will continue to come.

Churches usually served bus workers a big breakfast on Saturday mornings and then sent them out to spend much of the day contacting the riders of the bus routes. Churches quickly found that if members visited the kids on Saturday, those children would be ready to ride on Sunday morning. They also found that if the children weren't contacted on Saturday, they wouldn't be ready to ride on Sunday.

The principle was universal. If you contacted them, they would

> The fourth habit
> of the highly effective
> small group leader:
>
> *Contact group members
> regularly.*

continue to come, and if you did not contact them, they would not continue to come. It didn't matter if you had a rural route or one in the inner city. If you contacted them, they would continue to come. It took a lot of time and effort to contact every rider, every week. But many children came to know the Lord because of persistent weekly contacting by bus workers.

The principle of contacting not only works for the bus ministry, but it also works for small group leaders. If you continue to contact group members, they will continue to come.

Reasons for Contacting Your Members Regularly

Contacting helps your group grow

Once someone gets added to the roster, usually after the first visit, the highly effective leader will contact the person. This usually involves a short phone call thanking them for coming, asking how they liked the group, and inviting them to return. As these new ones come back and get connected to the group, the group grows.

We found the power of the principle of contacting when we started our church. We began with eleven people meeting in my basement, and the church grew to 100 in 6 months and 200 in 18 months. I called almost every family every week. I spend a few evenings a week and Saturday afternoon making these five-minute phone calls until the church got to an average attendance over 200. Then the five members of our leadership team divided the calling up between us. We found that the principle of contacting made the difference.

My two oldest sons started an evangelistic Bible study at their public school. They meet 45 minutes before school begins, every Wednesday morning. They gathered and grew the group to over 25 kids in a couple of months. Most of these kids are unchurched.

How did they do it? Every Tuesday, they talked to kids at school and every Tuesday night they got on the phone and made short phone calls. They found that the principle of contacting works. If they contacted their friends, they came, and if they did not contact them, they did not come.

My wife Cathy started a ladies small group recently. She grew and multiplied it into two groups in just a few weeks. How did she do it? She made a lot of phone calls and initiated many conversations with unconnected ladies at church. She understood the principle of contacting.

I lead a small group on Wednesday evenings. We have grown from a handful to nearly 30 people a week in a few months. How did we do it? We apply the principle of contacting. I contact new people, and my apprentices call all the attendees every week. If we contact them, they come.

Contacting increases your average weekly attendance

I have spoken in many churches throughout the country. Many pastors I preached for said, "We would have a big crowd, if only everybody was here. But some of our regulars are always gone." I have heard small group leaders say the same thing.

Several years ago, I wanted to prove a point. We had an "I'll be there" Sunday. The point was not to reach new people, but to get all of our regular attenders there for church all on the same week. About a month ahead of time, we called everyone in our church and asked them to mark their calendars and make a special effort to be there on "I'll be there" Sunday. We sent them a postcard reminding them of "I'll be there" Sunday, announced it for several weeks, and even gave people big buttons announcing, "I'll be there Sunday."

It was corny, tacky, and a lot of fun. It was also very effective. Attendance had been running about 750 a week. On "I'll be there" Sunday, we broke a thousand. And it was only our regular people. Attendance also stayed higher than 800 for the weeks following "I'll be there" Sunday.

Someone asked me, "Is it really that important for everyone to come to the group?" My answer was, "If it is not worth encouraging them to attend, why are you doing it?" I think our church services and small group meetings are worth attending. A person will benefit more by being there than they would by not being there. Therefore, I contact them to attend.

Regularly contacting small group members will increase the number of times they attend in a year. It provides a friendly form of accountability. This increases the number of times God can work in and through their lives during the small group meetings.

Contacting helps a shepherd know the state of his or her flock

Knowledge is essential for effective leadership. The better you know people, the better you can lead them. You can't 'grow' them if you don't 'know' them.

Someone in your small group may be going through a situation that he is reluctant to share with the group, but he will share it with you when you contact him outside of the group. It is amazing what people will tell you when you make contact with them over the phone, in person, or by e-mail. Use regular contacts to get to know them better and better. One of the biggest mistakes leaders make in selecting apprentices is failing to know them well enough. See the suggestions given later in this chapter for how to learn your people's hearts through contacting.

Contacting communicates care

Contacting says that you care. It says that you care enough to take the time to get in touch. It says that you care enough to find out why they were absent or what they think of the group. It says that you care enough to check on their prayer requests and to get to know them better.

Suggestions that Make Contacting Powerful

Ask them, "How may I pray for you?"

I have found asking people how to pray for them is one of the most valuable things I can do. This simple question unlocks the doors of their hearts. This is especially true when they know that you are listening carefully and will pray for them. People will share their deepest problems and greatest concerns with you.

Ask them, "What do you want God to do about this?"

I used to pray for people how I wanted to pray for them. Now, I ask what they want prayer for. This is important. Once, a lady asked me to pray for her mother who was very sick. I would have prayed for God to intervene and heal her, but that is not what the daughter wanted. She wanted God to take her mother home quickly and without any more pain because her mother was a Christian and had suffered greatly.

Asking what they want God to do helps you get to the heart of the matter. It helps you be on the same page so you can agree in prayer with them.

Then say, "Let's pray right now."

I used to tell people I would pray for them, and then I would forget. Now I pray for them right after they tell me their need, even if it is over the phone or in the lobby of the church. I have learned to 'strike while the iron is hot' by immediately taking the need to God.

I recently spoke with one of my small group leaders whose 85 year-old father is dying. At the end of our conversation, I prayed aloud for him, his father, and his family. He was choking back tears as we concluded the prayer. He thanked me and told me he was so glad to be in a church where he was loved.

Many times I have sensed the inrush of God's Spirit when I paused to pray aloud for someone's request. Hundreds of times, I have seen them wipe tears off their cheeks when I have finished. A simple prayer can draw us wonderfully near to God and each other.

Now ask, "Do you want to pray?"

If they are reluctant, do not push them to pray. If they tell me they don't want to pray, or if their silence tells me they do not want to, I usually say,

"That's okay. You don't have to. God knows your heart. Maybe next time."

But often they do appreciate the opportunity to express for themselves their need to God and their gratitude for your caring enough to pray. It also gives you added insight in their need and their prayer lives.

What to Talk About as Part of Your Regular Contact

A small group leader who contacts his members regularly has the opportunity to gradually grow in understanding them by asking questions. The key is showing interest. They should feel like you are genuinely hoping to know them better. They shouldn't feel like they are being interrogated. Use the following suggestions one or two at a time to get them to open up and share with you. You want to help them get beyond short answers and into really sharing themselves with you.

Over a period of time, you will come up with questions of your own. Until then, here are some of questions you can use:
- What are you up to this week?
- How are your kids doing?
- Do you like your job?
- On a scale of one to ten, how stressful was your week?
- Where did you grow up?
- How were you saved?
- When were you baptized?
- What do you like most about our church?
- What do you like best about our small group?
- What would you like to be different five or ten years from now?
- What area do you think God wants you to grow in this month?
- What are the things everyone says you are really good at?
- Have you ever thought of leading a group?

The Most Important Time to Make a Contact

It is great if you can contact everyone every week. But there are times when that is not possible. There are, however, certain times when a contact has the greatest impact and must be made. The highly effective small group leader is certain not to miss these times.

Soon after a first visit to your small group
This is often the key to getting visitors to come back for a second visit. It

lets them know that they were welcome. It gives you an opportunity to answer questions or clear up any confusion they might have. It also gives them a needed nudge to make the effort to come back.

Weekly for the first few weeks

I try to see that someone new is called every week for the first month or so. This will establish your relationship with them. It helps them make habit of coming to the group every week.

After an absence

Call people to let them know they were missed. If they were ill or having other problems, it lets you know how to pray for them. It encourages them not to allow missing group meetings to become a habit.

After the person has shared that they are going through a trial

This communicates that what they share in the group is taken seriously. It says that what is discussed in the group has meaning outside of the group in daily life. It shows that you care about them as people and not as numbers.

After a tense moment in the group

Occasionally, people argue or disagree in a group, often over little things. A touch by the leader soon after such a time tends to keep such things from building into problems down the road. Growing through conflict is the key to deepening relationships. Too many relationships remain superficial because conflict has been avoided or left unresolved. Do not miss this opportunity to deepen your relationship.

The Secrets Used by Highly Effective "Contactors"

- View the time you spend contacting as prime ministry time.
- Pray for Spirit-led direction as to what to say.
- Don't miss the key times mentioned earlier in this chapter.
- Pray about who God wants you to contact that week.
- Be positive about God, your church, and your small group.
- Be considerate of their time and schedule. If they are busy, be brief.
- Be sensitive to their mood. If they are willing to talk, take the time to listen. If not, don't push them.
- Have a place to record your contacts.
- Keep things that are shared in confidence, confidential.
- Be consistent. Try to see that everyone is contacted regularly.

- If they have shared a need with you, close the contact by praying for them.
- Use your apprentices and small group members to share the contacting load.
- Have a regular time scheduled each week to do your contacting. Build an hour or two of contacting into your weekly schedule and see what a difference it makes.

The Effective Small Group Leader Contacting Plan

My primary weekly contacting time(s):

_____

_____

The goal for the amount of time is _____ minutes a week.

I have a place to record contacts made weekly.

    Yes: _____ No: _____

My primary means of contacting is: (phone, home visit, e-mail, other) _____

The questions I will ask most frequently this week are

_____

_____

_____

_____

_____

_____

PREPARE:

Prepare for the Group Meeting

"Preparation is not my strong suit," Bill explains. Bill usually "flies by the seat of his pants" when it comes to his group. He says that he likes his group to be "free and spontaneous." Lately, attendance has begun to drop off. No one has invited any guests in awhile. The people in his group have begun to complain. They say the group is usually "just sharing Bill's pet peeves."

On the other hand, Dan and his apprentice Doug get together every Monday night to prepare for their Tuesday night small group meeting. The two hours they spend praying and preparing makes the one and a half hour meeting successful. Their group has grown. The group members look forward to coming every week and are not ashamed to invite guests. Dan and Doug have learned that a successful small group meeting does not just happen; it is the product of planning, prayer, and preparation.

The highly effective small group leader develops the habit of preparing for the group meeting. He carves out the time and puts in the effort to be ready for "the most important hour and a half of the week." He knows that the beginning of leadership is "knowing where you are going." He prepares each week so that he knows where the group is going when it meets. Weekly preparation keeps a group moving upward and onward for God.

The fifth habit
of the highly effective
small group leader:

Prepare for the group meeting.

Why Prepare?

Preparation gives God room to work

When a leader is well prepared, God has greater opportunity to work in the group. There are fewer distractions. Satan has fewer opportunities to get in and mess things up. The group flows more smoothly, allowing God to be the focus of the group.

Preparation increases confidence and faith

Highly effective leaders have learned that preparation is the key to approaching the group meeting with confidence. They spend the time preparing themselves and the agenda for the meeting. They know that the atmosphere will be made ready. They have confidence that they are ready to lead effective discussions of the Scriptures. They have thought carefully about the application of the discussion. During the group, they are free to enjoy the group and see God work in and through them and the group.

Preparation builds credibility

Group members naturally expect group leaders to lead. Most will gladly follow once they know that the leader knows where to go and how to get there. This allows the group members to relax and allows God to speak to and through them. They are not distracted or frustrated by a leader who is unprepared. They are more willing to invite guests.

Preparation increases quality

Ninety-nine percent of the time, the prepared leader will lead better than the unprepared one. They use the meeting time most wisely. The interpretation of the Bible will be more accurate. Potential sidetracks will be skillfully avoided. Distractions will be minimized. Taking the time to prepare will increase the quality of the group meeting.

Preparation reinforces the value of group life

People sense the value we place on something based on the time allotted it. If we fail to take the necessary time to prepare, the members will notice and have a diminished sense of the group's value. If a leader does not make it a priority to prepare, her members will not make it a priority to attend. If a leader does not show that she thinks of the group outside of the group, then members will not think to pray for one another and invite new people. However, when a leader shows that she is prepared, the value of the group is reinforced.

Preparing today is the secret of success tomorrow

Some group leaders get by week after week without really preparing. But in the long run, they will not reach maximum effectiveness. Effectiveness in the future is always the result of preparation in the past.

What to Prepare

Prepare Yourself

The most important element of preparation is personal preparation. Necessary areas of personal preparation revolve around several questions:

- Do I have any sin I need to confess?
- Am I allowing the Holy Spirit to be dominant in my life?
- Do I have a heart grateful for the opportunity to lead a group and all the people in it?
- Am I willing to apply the Word in my daily life?
- Are there any relationships I need to make right?

One of the greatest assets in personal preparation is fasting. It can be very beneficial to fast the day before or the day of your group. Fasting increases spiritual sensitivity. It frees God to be more active in answering our prayers. It cleanses our bodies and souls.

Another asset to personal preparation is praise and worship. Many effective leaders find it valuable to take a few minutes of their preparation time

My favorite way to prepare my heart

I generally fast the day of my group. Over my lunch hour, I close my eyes and imagine myself having a private appointment with God. I go to a park and spend the first few minutes drinking in the beauty of God's creation. Then I open up my prayer notebook and write out praises and personal prayer requests. I confess any sin. Then I pray for my group members by need and name. I conclude by praying through my group meeting. I like to lift every aspect of that night's meeting up to God in prayer.

Then I take a last deep drink of the beauty of the park. I leave and get a small snack. I enjoy my snack feeling wonderfully free, spiritually prepared, and close to God.

to lift their hearts to God in praise and worship. This may involve singing along with a CD or playing an instrument.

Prepare the Atmosphere

The atmosphere can make or break the meeting. It is nice when the group leader is not also the host. Whether you are the host or not, you need to ensure that the atmosphere is prepared to make the group meeting as good as possible. There are three main areas to prepare regarding the atmosphere:

- *The place.* The meeting place needs to be clean, comfortable, and spacious.
- *The music.* Two types of music aid a group meeting: first, quiet music playing while people are coming in and gathering; second, praise music for worship during the meeting.
- *The snack.* This can be a very important element of the group, especially for the first few weeks of a new group. People seem to feel more comfortable with a cup of coffee or a cookie in their hands. Having a simple snack can make the minutes before the group starts a more comfortable experience.

Prepare the Agenda for the Meeting

Welcome: 10-25 minutes

The three key elements in the welcome:

- *Snack and greeting on the way in the door.* The goal here is to make guests feel comfortable and glad they came. Have a friendly person greet them, take their coats, and lead them to the snack.
- *Group start and inclusive greeting.* When everyone, or almost everyone, has arrived, have people shake hands with or hug everyone in the group before finding a seat. The goal here is to help people feel warmth through appropriate touch. We live in a high tech, low touch world. Touch tears down barriers very quickly. I lead a group with many single adults who look forward to the hugs they get from our group as the only hugs they will get all week.
- *Ice-breaker.* The point of the icebreaker is to build the intimacy level of the group. The goal is to have everyone share something. The effective group leader wisely uses icebreakers to take the group to ever-deepening levels of intimacy.

The levels of intimacy and icebreakers:

- *Getting acquainted.* Have people share non-threatening things about themselves like favorite activities. People will learn that they have things in common with each other. Have people share about their past, such as childhood memories, teenage activities, and recent experiences. These icebreakers are effective for new groups or for times when several new people are present.

- *Getting spiritually acquainted.* Have the group members answer questions about their spiritual background, like if and where they went to church as a child and how they met Christ. Ask things like when they received their first Bible and what did they think of it. These questions take the group from a social level to a more spiritual level.
- *Affirmation.* After the group has gotten to know each other better, begin to have times of periodic affirmation. Have the group share things they appreciate about each other and are thankful for. This powerfully links hearts together.
- *Going deeper.* Let the group share their biggest points of pain and failure, both past and present. Have them give their testimonies. Good questions can reveal people's hurts, hearts, and histories. The key to getting beyond the surface is the leader's willingness to be open and honest. This is when the group begins to become a spiritual family.

Worship: 10-15 minutes

The elements of worship involve singing, praying, and saying thanks. Find out the things that your group can do and do them. Use variety to keep this fresh. Make sure you have everything you need to make this an effective time. This may include copies of song sheets and a musician or a sing-along worship CD. You can have people ready to tell God ten things they are thankful for, or five reasons to praise God.

Word: 30-45 minutes

Three key aspects of discussing the Word:
- *Questions that lead into the scripture or the topic of study.*
- *Questions that help people interact with the Scriptures.*
- *Ask the group members individually how they plan to apply the truth discussed.*

Witness: 10-30 minutes

Six work elements that work:
- *Pray for each other.*
- *Plan and pray for outreach.* Have people list the names of people they are inviting to the group or to church.
- *Plan to contact absentees.* Assign attendees to contact absentees. This

builds group community, and it makes it less of a leader-centered group and more of a member-centered group.

- *Plan social activities.* Always be talking about the next social activity on the horizon. Delegate various elements of making the social gathering a success.
- *Promote church activities.* The effective leader realizes that his group works best in concert with the local church. Take a minute or two each week to mention things like new members classes, church sponsored conferences and retreats, discipleship or Bible training classes, and small group leader training activities.
- *Pray for the church.* Cells are small parts of the larger body. Regularly take a few minutes to pray for the health of the body and the leaders of the church.

Things to remember as you prepare the agenda for the meeting:
- Vary the length and method of the various portions. Vary when you do the different elements.
- Flow naturally in and out of each element. Discuss things without officially announcing them. You don't have to say, "And now for our get acquainted icebreaker."
- End the meeting on time.

Prepare the Bible Discussion
- Pray over the Scripture.
- Study the Scripture.
  - Observation: What does the passage say?
  - Interpretation: What does it mean?
  - Application: How do we apply this to our lives?
- Determine connecting points with your group members.
- Develop appropriate introduction, discussion, and application questions.

Many churches require their leaders to follow an assigned curriculum that all of the groups use. Some supply the leaders with a worksheet based on the pastor's Sunday message. Some leaders use another type of Bible Study resource. Too many leaders spend all of their time preparing the Bible discussion. As a result, they have no time left for the other habits. You don't have to reinvent the wheel. Take the tools others have prepared, and spend a little time adapting them to your group.

Suggestions for Enhancing Your Preparation Time

- Prepare with your apprentice. This is great way to mentor them, and it allows for fresh perspectives and new ideas.
- Fast on the day you prepare.
- Have an established time and amount of time for preparation. Set a standing appointment each week to prepare for your group. Block out that time as sacred.
- Make use of the same place. Stock it with the tools you need. This will help you make better use of the time you have to prepare.

Secrets to Shorten Your Preparation Time

- Train and use your apprentice(s) and other members to lead meeting elements, especially the icebreaker and the prayer time.
- Follow a plan. Most groups use the plan of Welcome, Worship, Word, and Witness.
- Shorten Word discussion prep time by following a prewritten plan. You don't have time to be asking, "Well, what should we do this week?"
- Using resources provided by your church.
- Use already written lesson guides.

The Small Group Leader
Personal Preparation Chart

My weekly preparation time is _____

The amount of time is _____ minutes a week.

The place I will prepare is _____

Heart Preparation Questions:
- *Do I have any sin I need to confess?*
- *Is the Holy Spirit being allowed to be the dominant personality in my life?*
- *Do I have a grateful heart for the opportunity to lead a group and all the people in my group?*
- *Am I willing to live the Bible lesson in my daily life?*
- *Are their any relationships I need to make right?*

Meeting Agenda Preparation:
- Place
- Welcome
    - Snack
    - Greeting
    - Icebreaker
- Worship
    - Singing
    - Thanksgiving
    - Praise prayers
- Word
    - Introduction questions
    - Interaction discussion questions
    - Application questions
- Witness
    - Pray for each other
    - Pray for people we are inviting to group or church
    - Plan to contact absentees
    - Plan next social activity
    - Promotion of church activities
    - Prayer for church and church leaders

MENTOR:

Mentor Apprentice Leaders

Jim led a group for several years and did a good job. It was a strong group that met the needs of the members. Yet he never found an apprentice to mentor, so the group did not multiply. Then Jim had a stroke. He was physically unable to lead his group anymore. Since there was no one mentored to take his place, his group soon died. Looking back, Jim did everything right, except mentor an apprentice.

Rod led a group for several years and did a good job. It was a strong group that met the needs of the members. Rod mentored an apprentice named Scott. When Rod moved on to plant new groups, Scott took over. The group continued to grow. Over the years, Scott also mentored apprentices: Mike, Mark, Dave, Dale, and Jamal. Eventually they led their own groups. Many of their apprentices became leaders. Mike and Jamal went on to plant new churches. Rod and Scott made mentoring a priority and multiplied the group several times. Highly effective small group leaders make a habit of mentoring apprentices.

Years ago I ran track. One of my most enjoyable memories of track was competing in relays. The challenge of the relay is for four different runners, one after another, to get the baton around the track as fast as possible.

There are many similarities

The sixth habit
of the highly effective
small group leader:

Mentor apprentice leaders.

between Christian ministry and a relay race. In the relay, the baton must be passed from runner to runner. In Christianity, the gospel must be passed from person to person. In the relay, passing the baton requires concentration and communication. In Christianity, discipling people also takes concentration and communication.

In the relay, one fast runner cannot do it alone. It takes four runners working in concert in order to win. In Christianity, one gifted individual cannot do it all. It takes all of us doing our part to reach this world for Christ. In the relay, both the runner and the receiver need to do their part. In Christianity, both the one sharing the message and the person receiving it must do their part. In the relay, the race cannot be won unless the baton is passed successfully. In Christianity, the world will never be reached and the next generation will be lost unless we disciple others.

Jesus told his disciples to give their lives to passing on the baton.

Therefore go and make disciples of all nations, baptizing them in the name of the Father and of the Son and of the Holy Spirit, and teaching them to obey everything I have commanded you. And surely I am with you always, to the very end of the age.
(Matthew 28:19-20)

Paul told Timothy to pass on the baton. Interestingly, he describes one 'generation' passing it on to the next. There are four levels in just one verse:

And the things you have heard me say in the presence of many witnesses entrust to reliable men who will also be qualified to teach others. (2 Timothy 2:2)

- *Me:* Paul
- *You:* Timothy
- *Reliable men:* Timothy's apprentices
- *Others:* The apprentices of Timothy's apprentices

Paul understood that in ministry there is no lasting success without a successor. One of the non-negotiable habits of a highly effective small group leader is mentoring apprentices, raising up leaders to lead future groups.

Mentoring Is . . .

Cooperating with God in raising up an apprentice to become a highly effective small group leader

In this chapter when we speak of mentoring, we are talking specifically about small group leaders developing other small group leaders. This may sound overwhelming, but raising up spiritual reproducers is the heart of God. All you have to do is cooperate with Him in the process.

Following the examples of Jesus and Paul

A study of the gospels reveals that mentoring was Jesus' method. The goal of the Christian life is to be like Jesus. In no way is a Christian more like Jesus then when he or she is making disciples and raising up leaders. Before Jesus told his disciples to make disciples, He did it Himself. Men were His method. As we shall see in this chapter, Jesus spent his ministry life mentoring future leaders.

Mentoring was Paul's method too. Paul told the Corinthians to follow him as he followed Christ. One of the ways Paul followed Christ was mentoring leaders. When he was killed, the ministry did not stop. Timothy, Silas, Titus, and others carried on.

A great way to love others

When I think of the obligation to love others, I get a bit overwhelmed because I know hundreds of people. Where do I concentrate my love? I have learned to concentrate my efforts to shower love on the people I am mentoring. I have found that mentoring apprentices is concentrating your 'love' on a few in order to reach the many.

Love is doing what is best for others. Nothing is as good for others as helping them succeed. Mentoring in its purest sense is empowering others to succeed.

The means of multiplying yourself

How many times have we wished we could be at two places at one time? Mentoring is the only way a busy person can minister in more than one place at a time. For example, fifteen years ago I started one group. I could only be in that one group. Yet I mentored the people in that group to become multiplying small group leaders. Many of those in that group have spent time the last few years raising up group leaders. Today there are nearly 100 groups from that initial group. So now, in a sense, I can be at 100 places at a time!

The way one ordinary person can reach thousands

Never underestimate the power of multiplication. As we saw in chapter one, the first few 'generations' or levels are not overly impressive. One becomes 2, and 2 becomes 4. But as reproducers raise-up reproducers the impact multiplies. Slowly 4 becomes 8, then 16, 32 and 64. Then the impact explodes as 64 become 128, then 256, and 512. And by the tenth 'generation' of leaders, one has become 1024!

You say, "I could never minister to a thousand people." But if you are an effective small group leader, you can mentor someone else to become a leader. And by mentoring one highly effective leader at a time, you can eventually minister to thousands through the ministry of the leaders you have trained. Effective mentors understand that they will never have multiplied results until they multiply themselves into other leaders.

The heart of disciple-making

When Jesus gave the command to 'make disciples,' He wasn't just commanding us to teach people the Bible. He was commanding us to disciple people to disciple others. We need to disciple them to do ministry. Too much of what is called discipleship is only about learning information. Mentoring is about helping apprentices take information and use it to lead others.

A way to maintain godly accountability

Mentoring works when there is accountability between the mentor and apprentice. This accountability extends from the expectations of learning to leading a group to personal devotions and dealing with blind spots. Mentoring creates a natural accountability relationship.

Letting go of ministry in order to let others minister

People fail to see their ministries grow because they hang on to them too tightly. They fall in love with doing ministry. They enjoy meeting people's needs and seeing them grow. Sometimes they even get their self-esteem from being needed by the members of their group.

The problem with doing ministry by yourself is that it does not develop other 'ministers'. The ministry stops with you. Effective mentoring involves letting go of ministry in order to let others minister. It lets others get in on the fun of seeing God use them to change people's lives. Effective mentors learn to enjoy the ministry success of others as much or more than their own ministry successes.

Saying, "No" to the urgent in order to say, "Yes" to the potential of the important

Satan does everything he can to keep us from Christ. Once we are in Christ he does everything he can to keep us from ministering. Once we are ministering, he does all he can to keep us from mentoring. This is because he sees the awesome potential mentoring has to expand the kingdom of God. One of his favorite ways to keep us from mentoring is to get us so caught up with the tyranny of the urgent that we miss the potential of the important. We get so caught up in the urgency of doing ministry that we fail to mentor leaders, the area of true importance. Effective small group leaders make the choice to make mentoring a priority even in the midst of everything else they are doing.

The most lasting part of small group leadership

I have led groups for over 20 years. The thing I look back on is not the groups I have led but the leaders I have developed, especially those who are effectively mentoring others. I count church leaders, pastors, and full-time missionary church planters among the people I have had the privilege of mentoring. Their ministry has continued long after I have moved on to new areas of ministry.

Seven Steps for Raising Up Multiplying Leaders and Reproducing Reproducers

1. Demonstrate what you hope to reproduce.

You have to produce before you can reproduce. It takes an effective leader to make an effective leader. Students emulate what they see more than what we say. The person who raises up highly effective small group leaders who will live the eight habits is the leader who lives the eight habits himself.

Personal Inventory Of the Eight Habits:
- I have the dream of and a target date for multiplying my group.
- I spend quality and quantity time in prayer daily.
- I set aside time to invite new people to my group.
- I contact the members of my group regularly.
- I spend time each week preparing for our group meeting.
- I have an apprentice who I am mentoring to become an effective group leader.

- I lead my group to have regular social gatherings.
- I follow a plan for personal growth and fitness.

2. Discover potential leaders.

As you grow as leader, be on the look out for potential leaders. Begin with the mindset that everyone can become a leader. When Joel Comiskey studied 700 effective small group leaders in eight distinct cultures, he "discovered that the potential to lead a growing, successful, small group does not reside with the gifted, the educated, or those with vibrant personalities. The answer, rather, is hard work."[1]

See who has a heart for the work. One way to discover potential leaders is to see who has a heart for small group ministry. Give out various responsibilities and see who seizes the opportunity. Ask people in your group to contact others in the group who are absent. Watch to see who volunteers to do it and who actually follows through. Those who will do the work distinguish themselves as potential leaders.

Pray. Jesus told his disciples to "pray for the Lord of the harvest to raise up laborers for the harvest" (Matthew 9:38). As you pray for your group members daily, ask God to show you who to invite to become an apprentice. He will help you see people through the eyes of a mentor. He will show you who He wants you to mentor.

Some people say they just can't find an apprentice. This is hard for me to believe. Every time I have asked God to give me someone to disciple, He has provided. For example, during the last five months of my sophomore year in college, He answered prayer and gave me a handful of men to help grow spiritually. By the next year, they all had their own groups. Start by discipling a few people and the potential apprentices will become obvious.

Narrow the field by looking for people with the highest potential to be developed by you. Everyone can become a leader, but not everyone is ready to become an apprentice under you. When looking for potential apprentices, apply the Three C's:

- *Compatibility.* When Jesus selected his twelve he "called to him those he wanted" (Mark 3:13). He knew that mentoring would mean spending time together, so he selected those he wanted to spend time with. Mentoring requires spending time together, and in our busy world, this won't happen unless you get along with and like each other. Choose people you enjoy being with and who enjoy being with you.
- *Character.* Paul told Timothy to select leaders on the basis of character (1 Timothy 3:1-8). When it comes to the essential elements of character needed to become a leader look for people of faith and people of F.A.I.T.H:
  - *Faithful.* The prime quality Paul told Timothy to look for in

potential leaders was faithfulness (2 Tim.2:2). Take note of people who make the group meetings a priority. Key an eye on those who are faithful in personal devotions. Be on the lookout for those who follow through on assignments.

- *Available.* You cannot mentor someone you can't spend time with. Select apprentices who are available to get together with you on a regular basis.
- *Initiative.* Look for those who seek to help out, who want to get more involved, and who can take an idea and run with it. One definition of leadership is "taking the initiative to see that what needs to get done gets done."
- *Teachable.* You cannot be of much help to someone who already thinks he knows it all. Find people who are hungry to learn and pour your life into them.
- *Honest, Open, and Transparent.* People who are not really open and honest will become increasingly frustrating to work with. Select a person who does not try to hide and can admit sins, faults, failures, and mistakes. Choose people who will admit it when they are wrong.
• *Competency.* Through Jethro, God told Moses to select able men, or people who could do the job (Exodus 18:21). While everyone can become a leader, not everyone will be capable of leading right away. Jesus told the demoniac of Gadara to go home and minister because he was not ready for the rigorous commitment Jesus was asking of His disciples (Mark 5:19).

Maybe their jobs or family situations are limiting them right now. Maybe they need to grow in their understanding of the Bible. Maybe they need to develop their people skills.

3. Deepen your relationship with potential leaders.

Author Bill Hull stated, "If you are not willing to get truly close to a few people for Christ then you will not have the full impact that is vital for discipleship."[2]

As you discover potential leaders, make the effort to get to know them better. Start to spend time with them outside of the group. The better your relationship with a person, the more effective your ministry will be to and with that person. You need to be close enough not only to recognize his or her weaknesses, but also to be trusted when you point them out.

Two of the best ways to deepen relationships:
• *Pray together.* Nothing knits people closer together than quality time spent around the throne of God. This reveals her heart to you. It exposes her to your heart for God and your ministry. God works

when we pray together.
- *Play together.* Capitalize on every opportunity to spend time together outside of small group ministry settings. There are many things you can do together. Go out and do them! It could be sharing meals together, visiting in each other's homes, attending an event together, or exercising together. What you do is not important as long as you are doing it together.

4. Describe the vision.

Once you have found someone whom you believe God wants you to invite to become an apprentice, get together and describe the vision. The reason some fail to recruit and mentor effective leaders successfully is that they overlook the need of describing the vision. People will not lay down their lives for a program, but they will lay down their lives for a vision.

Early and often, the mentor needs to share the vision of changing the world by becoming an effective small group leader. Nehemiah kept the people working in spite of intense pressure because he regularly shared the vision of rebuilding the walls of Jerusalem. If an apprentice lacks motivation, it is because he or she lacks vision.

Some elements of the vision to share:
- *The vision of the church.*
- *The vision of multiplying leaders and groups.*
- *The vision of the potential to make a difference.*

Once, a journalist was watching the building of a great cathedral in Europe. There were two bricklayers who caught his attention. One worked carelessly and grudgingly. The other worked with great energy and precision. When he asked them, "What are you doing?" The first shrugged and said, "Laying brick." The second smiled and said, "Building a great cathedral." Vision made the difference.

5. Determine the commitment to be made.

When Jesus called his disciples, he explained the commitment involved. He let them see what He was all about. Then, He gave them the vision of fishing for men. Fishing for men involved two commitments: their commitment was to follow Him, and His commitment was to make them fishers of men (Mark 1:16-20).

Too many well-intentioned group leaders struggle in developing apprentices because they don't ask for commitment. Remember, if you don't ask for commitment, you won't get it.

Explain your commitment to them:
- Set the PACE for them:
  - **P**ray for them.
  - **A**vailable to them.
  - **C**ontact and Communicate with them.
  - **E**xample progressing Christian living for them.
- Train them to do what it takes to lead an effective group meeting, like Welcome, Worship, etc.
- Train them to live the eight habits of an effective small group leader.

Explain their commitments as an apprentice small group leader:
- Their commitment to be equipped by meeting with you and the small group coach. Have them commit to coming to group early and staying late so you can discuss meeting elements and events with them.
- Their commitment to fulfill the role of an apprentice by beginning to practice the eight habits of the effective small group leader. Ask them to begin living the eight habits for six months or until ready to lead on their own.
- Their commitment to mentor others. Paul told Timothy to commit himself to train faithful men who would train others (2 Timothy 2:2). Build in the expectation of reproducing reproducers from the very beginning. Help them be committed to mentoring multipliers. Pray with them about their apprentices before they become apprentices.

6. Develop Them.

Once they have accepted the commitment to become apprentices, train them to lead groups. We must never ask people to do something they are not trained to do. There are four discernable steps in the training process of developing leaders. These are visible in the ministry of Jesus and the twelve and in the ministry of Barnabas and Paul.
- *Model it.* Have them watch as you do ministry, just as Jesus did with His disciples (Matthew 9:32-38). Let them see a highly effective small group leader in action. When Paul and Barnabas were sent out to minister, Barnabas was the leader. Barnabas was doing the ministry and Paul was observing. Note how they are listed as "Barnabas and Paul" (Acts 13:1-5).
- *Mentor it.* Have them minister while you watch, assist, correct, and encourage, as Jesus did with His disciples (Matthew 10:1). Not long into their journey, Barnabas moved over to give Paul the opportunity to lead. Note that they now were listed as "Paul and Barnabas" (Acts 13:6ff).

- *Motivate it.* Have them do it as you encourage from a distance, as Jesus did when he sent them out two by two without Him (Matthew 10:5). Similarly, when Paul and Barnabas prepared for another missionary journey, Paul was ready to go on his own. (Acts 15:36-41).

- *Multiply it.* The original disciples multiplied out to a total of 70 (Luke 10:1), then perhaps 500 (1 Corinthians 15:6). After Jesus ascended to heaven, the number of disciples began to multiply to 3,000 (Acts 2:41), then 5,000 men (Acts 4:4), then so many that the Bible just says the number was multiplied (Acts 6:7).

   In similar fashion, Paul was soon ministering without the help of Barnabas and beginning to take others through the mentoring process like Silas (Acts 15:39-41) and Timothy (Acts 16:1-3). By Acts 17:14, Paul went off to minister and left Timothy and Silas to minister in Berea on their own.

7. Deploy them.

A leader has not fully succeeded until she has deployed successors. Once an apprentice has gone through the other six steps, it is time to release him or her into ministry. This is one of the most exciting times of your ministry. You get to see someone you have led and trained leading and training others. This is a source of immense joy.

In the ministry of Jesus we see the ultimate act of deployment when Jesus gave his disciples the Great Commission and then left them to fulfill it as he left the earth (Acts 1:8-9). From that point on, He was no longer physically with them.

Three Ways to Birth a New Group

While there are several ineffective ways to birth new groups, there is no one right way to birth a group. Any form of these three basic methods can be very effective, as can a combination of them.

Multiply: Two groups of equal size multiply from a parent group

The vision of multiplication is shared. A new leader and/or leadership team develops. Relationships are developed. Group members are given the option of staying with the original leaders or being a part of the new group. The goal is to have a nearly equal number of people in both groups.

Launch: A core group from a parent group launches a new group

As in option one, the vision of multiplication is shared. A new leadership team develops. Group members are given the option of staying with the original leaders or being a part of the new group. However, having equal halves is not necessarily the goal. The new leaders understand that the new group will be launched without many people from the parent group.

Plant: One person from a parent group plants a new group while others remain as a part of the parent group

The planter can be either the original leader or a new leader.

We coordinate our church around three small group seasons: Fall (September, October, November, December); Winter (January, February, March and April) and Summer (May, June July and August.). We use one Sunday morning Celebration at the beginning of each season to enlist all church attendees into groups. This is the natural time for us to start most new groups. We find the best time to launch and plant groups is fall. For us, the best time to multiply is early winter.

Mentoring Suggestions

- Never do ministry alone.
- Take full advantage of all the training opportunities your church offers.
- Be constantly on the look out for new leaders.
- Talk of leadership as a privilege, not a burden.
- Don't put yourself on a pedestal or good people will shy away from leadership.
- Give responsibilities before you ask someone to consider being a leader.
- Always consult with those above you before you give any titles.
- Realize that failing to mentor will always mean failing to multiply.
- Do not release leaders until they have a good chance of success.
- As you move through the group cycle, have your ministry role decrease and your apprentice's role increase.
- Give lavish affirmation and encouragement to apprentices each step of the way.

Multiplication Suggestions

Talk about multiplying early and often

Start from the very first week. Describe the fact that one of the purposes of the group is to raise-up leaders who will be sent out to lead new groups. At least monthly, pray in the group about the new groups to be birthed from your parent group. Remember people are negative toward what they have not been prepared for. Keep the group informed of the plans and progress each step along the way.

Talk about multiplying in positive terms

Do not speak of "breaking up" the group, "splitting" the group, or "dividing" the group. Instead talk about "birthing" new groups, "launching" new groups, "multiplying" groups, and "raising up" new groups and leaders.

Talk about multiplying in terms of the big picture

In our metropolitan area there are over 850,000 unchurched people. Over 200,000 people live within convenient driving distance of our weekend worship services. Every new group that is born lowers the number of unchurched people. When we talk about birthing new groups, we talk about reaching more of the 850,000 people who are unchurched.

I find that when we begin to speak of multiplying, people often resist. Then we ask how many of them were not in church or our group a year ago. This is usually quite a few. Then we ask, "What if the people who were in our group a year ago had been too selfish to give up their place in this group? Where would you be now?"

Pray about the best method and the best timing for multiplying

It is possible to make the right decision at the wrong time. Maybe the group is ready to multiply, but the new leader(s) are not. Or maybe the new leader(s) are ready, but the group is not. Or maybe it is a poor season to launch. For us, summer is usually not a good season to launch. Pray about finding the best timing for multiplication.

Set a date for multiplying

Setting a date for multiplying is essential in achieving the dream of multiplying your group. According to Joel Comiskey's survey of 700 multiplying small group leaders,

> *Cell leaders who know their goal — when their groups will give birth — consistently multiply their groups more often than leaders who don't know. In fact, if a cell leader fails to set goals the cell members can clearly remember, he has about a 50-50 chance of multiplying his cell. But if the leader set goals, the chance of multiplying increases to three of four.*[3]

Celebrate the new birth

When the small group is ready to give birth, have a party and invite friends. Ask the small groups pastor to preside over a special time of prayer, sending out the new group(s) and leader(s). It is a great opportunity to recast the vision for multiplying. Some churches may make this a part of their worship celebrations to make a visual statement of their priorities and vision.

The Small Group Leader Personal Mentoring Chart

The person(s) I am mentoring as an apprentice to lead future groups is

(are) _____

_____

_____

Our weekly mentoring time(s) is (are) _____

_____

_____

The amount of time is _____ minutes a week.

The place is _____

_____

The step of mentoring I need to be working on with them is

_____

_____

_____

_____

_____

FELLOWSHIP:

Plan Group Fellowship Activities

7

Tim's group started well but lost momentum. People grew less and less excited about coming to group; attendance became sporadic. He shared his frustration with his small group coach. His coach asked a simple question, "How did your last group social activity go?"

Tim blushed and stammered, "We haven't had any."

His coach gave him a few pointers and suggestions for possible social activities. As a result, Tim committed to having one. That week, he shared the idea with his group. The ladies perked up when he mentioned a social gathering, and the guys got interested when he mentioned a Super Bowl party. The conversation took on a spiritual tone when he mentioned using it to attract some new people to the group.

The gathering was a great success. The group regained morale and momentum. Three new people visited, and Tim learned the value of social gatherings and fellowship. Highly effective small group leaders take full advantage of the power of social gatherings.

> The seventh habit of the highly effective small group leader:
>
> *Plan group fellowship activities.*

The Power of Social Gatherings for Fellowship

Social gatherings increase excitement, interest, and involvement

I have understood the value of social gatherings, but I hate to plan them. A few years ago, I noticed that my group was getting a little stale. I realized we hadn't had any social gatherings in a while. So I suggested that we have an "I Hate Winter Party" during the first half of the meeting next week. They all laughed because it is cold and snowy in Ohio in the winter. But I convinced them I was serious, and we planned it.

I told them we would turn the heat up and suggested that everyone wear summer clothes, drink lemonade, and eat picnic foods. A very quiet lady in my group, named Diane, became quite animated at the mention of a party. She lit up and said, "I love parties. Could I help plan it?"

That party was very successful and we set a high attendance record. People laughed and opened up on a whole new level. In the weeks after the party, they began to invite more friends "because the group is so much fun and the people are so nice."

Best of all, the fellowship activity not only re-ignited my group, but also ignited the previously quiet Diane. She became consistent in group attendance and hosted most of our get-togethers. She found a niche of service and even got her boyfriend involved in the group.

Social gatherings attract new people

Many times, friends or family members are attracted to the group through social gatherings. Often, they will not attend a church service or a group but will attend a social gathering. Use social gatherings to allow these people to see that Christians can have fun. Let them see the love and closeness that those in the group have found. Once the skeptical family member or friend gets to know a few Christians, it is much easier for them to take the next step of attending the group or a church service.

Social gatherings allow more opportunities to practice real fellowship

The New Testament concept of fellowship comes from the Greek word *koinonia*. It means sharing together. A good small group meeting helps people share worship, their burdens, prayer, and discussion of the Word. A good social gathering allows them to share even more areas of their lives together.

I will never forget the day our men's group took our wives and children canoeing. This trip not only allowed my men's group to share our families together, but also helped us see each other in a different setting. Many of us got to share the adversity of tipping over in white water. Many in the group got the privilege of rescuing me from drowning. Our group drew closer together through the shared experience.

During a good social gathering, people discuss things that never seem to come up in a group meeting. People learn to share in different ways. I remember going to visit a lady in the hospital one night. I got off the elevator to hear a happy ruckus going on in the lobby. I turned the corner to find her seated in the lobby surrounded by her small group. Since she could not come to group, they had brought the group to her. They not only shared life on a different level that night, but they also had a great testimony to all the people who overheard the fun going on.

Sharing in the group usually starts out superficial. One way to take people to a different level quickly is through a social gathering. Members get to see each other as "real people." Going rafting or playing softball allows the group members to see sides of one another that would rarely be seen in the group meeting.

Social gatherings can create opportunities to obey the 'one another' commands of the New Testament

The New Testament records 21 "one another" commands. These are the commands given to believers telling us how God expects us to treat one another as members of His family. They tell us how to share together in fellowship.

The umbrella command of the "one another" commands is to love one another (John 13:34-35; Romans 13:8; 1 Peter 1:22; 1 John 3:11; 3:23; 4:7; 4:11-12; 2 John 1:5). The expression of such love is embodied in the 20 other "one another" commands. While many of these commands can be fulfilled in a group meeting, they can also be fulfilled in different and deeper ways in social settings. Look at this list and think how these could be practiced in settings outside the group meeting.

- Honor one another. (Romans 12:16)
- Speak to one another with psalms. (Ephesians 5:19)
- Live in harmony with one another. (Romans 12:16)
- Submit to one another. (Ephesians 5:21)
- Stop judging one another. (Romans 14:13)
- Bear with and forgive one another. (Colossians 3:13)
- Accept one another. (Romans 15:7)
- Teach and admonish one another. (Colossians 3:16)
- Instruct one another. (Romans 15:14)
- Encourage one another. (1 Thessalonians 5:11; Hebrews 3:13; 10:25)
- Greet one another. (Romans 16:16; 1 Corinthians 16:20; 2 Corinthians 13:12; 1 Peter 5:14)
- Spur one another on to love and good works. (Hebrews 10:24)

- Agree with one another. (1 Corinthians 1:10)
- Do not slander one another. (James 4:11)
- Serve one another. (Galatians 5:13)
- Offer hospitality to one another. (1 Peter 4:9)
- Bear with one another. (Ephesians 4:32)
- Clothe selves in humility toward one another. (1 Peter 5:5)
- Be kind, compassionate, and forgiving to one another. (Ephesians 4:32)
- Walk in the light and fellowship with one another. (1 John 1:7)

Social gatherings create opportunities for further discipleship

Some of Jesus' greatest moments with His disciples were not in formal settings but in social ones. These social settings created the most teachable moments to display or convey tremendous truth. Consider some of these examples.

- At a wedding. (John 2:1-10)
- At a dinner party. (Luke 5:29-32; 7:36-48)
- On a boat ride. (Luke 8:22-25)
- At a funeral. (John 11:17-44)
- Picking grain. (Matthew 12:1-8)
- At a holiday meal. (Matthew 26:17-28)
- On a walk. (Luke 24:13-27)

Jesus used every opportunity to disciple His group. Some things came up in social gatherings that would not have come up at any other time. Some leaders miss valuable opportunities to disciple their groups when they fail to capitalize on social gatherings. Highly effective leaders utilize the value of social gatherings to disciple their groups.

Social gatherings help knit new people to the group and the church

Research shows that if new people at a church or group do not make seven friends within the first seven weeks of attendance, they will not stay. Small groups and social gatherings are the natural solution to this situation. Use social gatherings as an opportunity to help new people make friends with the others in your group. Have some type of social gathering at least every seven weeks, and focus on getting new people there.

Suggestions for Effectively Using Social Gatherings and Fellowship Activities

Think 'togetherness'

The point of these gatherings is fellowship on a different level. Share together. It really doesn't matter what you do, so long as you all do it together. I had a men's group that over the course of a year did such diverse activities as shoot each other on a paint ball course, go bowling, play basketball, play board games, have a prayer walk, attend a professional baseball game, and watch a movie. The point was not what we were doing; it was the fact that we were doing it together.

Use variety

Don't do the same thing every time. Mix it up. Use a variety of social gatherings. Use some for service projects, some to do team building, and some purely for fun. One month, clean up a widow's lawn, and the next month, go bowling. Have some events that are just for the guys and some just for the ladies. Include the children in some but not in others. Try to have one or two big social activities a year with several smaller ones in between.

Use the power of food

I used to wonder why God designed us with the need to spend time each day eating. It seemed like such a waste of time. Yet, He also designed us to be social creatures. When there is the combination of the human drive to eat and the need for social interaction, the power of food to enhance fellowship becomes clear.

Have a group with no food and in some minds it is a meeting. People are not overly excited about it. Have food and it is more exciting. Have unusual or special food and it is a party. People want to come and will bring their friends. When you plan social gatherings and fellowship activities, use the power of food to enhance fellowship.

Do not do all the work yourself; delegate!

Your leadership is not measured by what you can do; it is measured by what you can get done through others. There are people with gifts of organizing and hospitality. Turn them loose. Appreciate, recognize, and support them. Let them do the work.

Plan ahead

Have activities coming every month or so. Let people know when the activities will be ahead of time, and remind them weekly in the group meeting. Plan far enough ahead so that people setting up the activity feel like they have enough time to get ready for it and so people in the group can work it into their schedules. Create and print out a calendar of events.

Combine activities with group meetings

I live in a suburb of a large city. Everyone is busy. I have found it wise to combine an activity with the group meeting on occasion. Our group meets from 7:05 to 8:40. When we have a "party," we use it in place of the icebreaker and worship and still have time to study the Word and pray. These gatherings help build attendance and morale. Even though they take a minimal amount of planning and effort, they make a maximum impact. They make the group fun.

Relax, have fun, and enjoy each other

Sometimes relationships are built most easily in less structured settings. Don't worry about every nuance of the activity going perfectly. Focus on being with the others and enjoying their presence. Remind people that the goal is to have fun and be together. Watch as defenses come down and people open up as they laugh together.

Possible Social Gatherings and Fellowship Activities

The following is a list of 52 possible fellowship gatherings that groups in my church have used through the years. This list is not exhaustive. There are some great activities that are not on it. Some of these activities will fit your group; others will not. It is meant to serve as an idea starter for your group so that you can come up with your own activities and plans for implementing them. The key is to do it together.

1. Have a party the first half of the group meeting. Have everyone bring food, and use the time to talk and laugh and maybe play some games.
2. Have a group picnic.
3. Go to a baseball game.
4. Clean a widow's house.
5. Serve in the church nursery.
6. Play softball.
7. Have a married couples' date night.

8. Visit and hold a worship service in a nursing home.

9. Attend a Christian conference or seminar.

10. Go for a bike ride.

11. Camp together.

12. Mow and clean up a retired man's lawn.

13. Serve food to the poor and homeless in a soup kitchen.

14. Serve as greeters or parking lot attendants for weekend services.

15. Have a cookout.

16. Go bowling.

17. Play volleyball.

18. Pass out Bibles door-to-door.

19. Take a short-term missions trip.

20. Go out to eat at a nice restaurant.

21. Put a roof on a disabled man's house.

22. Take Christmas dinner and gifts to a needy family.

23. Watch a group member perform in a concert or play.

24. Go for a hike.

25. Help a group member move.

26. Have a holiday party.

27. Watch a special TV program.

28. Play board games.

29. Have a theme party and dress accordingly.

30. Visit a museum.

31. Go Christmas caroling.

32. Play soccer.

33. Go shopping.

34. Have a birthday party.

35. Visit a group member in the hospital.

36. Have an international dinner with a missionary.

37. Have a scavenger hunt.

38. Have an all-night prayer meeting.

39. Attend the funeral for the family member of a group member.

40. Play basketball.

41. Serve as counselors or sponsors at a youth activity.

42. Paint a needy person's home.

43. Play Frisbee golf.

44. Bake cookies.

45. Serve in children's church together.

46. Go canoeing or rafting.

47. Have a house warming or dedication party.

48. Go to a concert.

49. Run an obstacle course.
50. Play paintball.
51. Have a pool party.
52. Go on a prayer walk.

The Small Group Leader's Fellowship Activity Planning chart

1. Read the list of 52 possible fellowship activities. Circle several that sound fun to you.

2. Plan the first one and carry it off successfully.

3. Before the second one, read the list to the group. Ask the group if they have any ideas for any others they would like to try.

4. Plan a tentative schedule with an average of one event per month. Have a combination of simple activities and more involved ones.

5. Get a team of people to own the gatherings or maybe ask different individuals to own each one. Let them take the ball and run with it.

GROW:

Be Committed to Personal Growth

Wes was a great small group leader. A whirling dervish of activity, he was great at inviting new people and contacting his members. He raised up several apprentices who became effective group leaders as well. He loved to minister and poured himself out in service.

After a few years, he began to feel empty. His group was growing stale. At the same time, he was experiencing some problems with his health and his weight. Things were not always happy at home, and his children were beginning to wander spiritually and make poor choices. He felt tired all the time, and his sunny personality disappeared. He was losing his passion for God and wondered what was wrong.

His small group coach challenged him to set up a personal growth plan. It included activities to keep his spiritual tanks full. It addressed his diet and exercise needs. The plan included regular time spent investing in his marriage and kids. He began to grow again. Within a few months, Wes felt much better. Things began to pick up at home. His ministry was rekindled, and his effectiveness reached an entirely new level.

The highly effective small group leader must learn the value of investing in his personal growth or he'll never be able to serve as a small group leader over the long haul.

> The eighth habit of the highly effective small group leader:
>
> *Be committed to personal growth.*

Insights into Personal Growth

Personal growth is expected of us by God

God expects us to grow. He expects us to be constantly developing our character and our skills to minister effectively for Christ.

We need to pay attention to personal growth because God expects us to. He commands us to grow saying, "But grow in the grace and knowledge of our Lord and Savior Jesus Christ" (2 Peter 3:18). Paul told Timothy that taking time to train oneself in godliness is a key element of an effective ministry for Christ. He commanded him to be diligent so others would see His progress (1 Timothy 4:7,15).

Personal growth is the fountainhead of group change and growth

Most things are out of our control. About the only thing you can directly improve is yourself. When you improve yourself the situation will improve. When you grow as a leader, you allow God to grow your group and your people through you. You could say that the key to changing the group is changing the leader. Grow the group by growing the leader. Improve the group by improving the leader.

Personal growth prevents decline

I used to live in central Virginia on the edge of the Blue Ridge Mountains. One winter, we had an unusually large amount of snow and ice. One evening, I was trying to visit some people from my church, and it was snowing. I was still a fairly inexperienced driver and had to drive up a steep hill to get to their house.

I did not have much momentum when I got to the hill, so I stopped about a third of the way up. Then, a frightening thing happened. Instead of staying still, I began to slide back down all the way to the bottom. The second time, I got a little more speed before I hit the hill, but stopped about two-thirds of the way up. When I stopped, I did not stay still. I slid all the way back down to the bottom. The third time, I kept moving forward no matter what, and eventually I made it to the top.

That night, I learned two valuable lessons. First, if you are on a slippery slope, don't stop your forward progress. Second, if you live in central Virginia, buy snow tires.

Nothing in our universe, except God, stays the same. Everything is either developing or declining. Our personal, spiritual lives are growing or dying. If we don't aggressively press on, we will soon be sliding back.

It has been observed that, "Most of us must learn a great deal every day in order to keep ahead of what we forget."

The highly effective small group leader understands that unless he is intentionally making progress in his personal, spiritual life he will soon begin to decline. The leadership skills that worked at one level are ineffective at another.

Personal growth is something you must do yourself

An Irish proverb says, "You have to do your own growing, no matter how tall your grandfather is." Paul told Timothy, "train yourself to be godly" (2 Timothy 4:7). No one else could do it for him.

As Christians, we understand that we are not the victims of our environment. We have learned that what we are is more the product of our decisions than our conditions. God says that we will have to give an account of ourselves when we stand before Him (Romans 14:12). No one else is responsible for our personal growth. No one else can grow for us, learn for us, and improve for us. We have to grow, learn, and develop for ourselves.

Personal growth is the key to staying sharp and effective

A man was hired to cut down trees as a lumberjack. The more trees he cut down, the more he was paid. He was big, strong, in great shape, and willing to work hard.

The first day, he got right to work and cut down ten trees. The next day, he went right to work and cut down eight. The third day, he was only able to fell six trees. The fourth day, his total was four. The fifth day, he only cut down three. At the end of the day, he was discouraged. He had worked just as long and hard each day, yet his total kept declining.

He noticed that during the same week, an experienced lumberjack had dropped nine trees each day. The new lumberjack approached the experienced one and said, "Let me ask you two questions: First, how did you do the same amount each day and my total kept declining? Second, I got right to work each morning and you didn't. What were you doing?"

The lumberjack smiled and said, "I can answer both questions with one answer. Each morning, I take time to sharpen my saw."

I have read through the Bible several times, but I find that I need to get up each day and read a few chapters in order to stay sharp. I have read many books in my life, yet I find that I need to read a book every week or so to keep focused. I want to stay sharp and useful for God.

Personal growth is a life-long process, not a short-term commitment

The Apostle Paul gave this testimony:

Not that I have already obtained all this, or have already been made perfect, but I press on to take hold of that for which Christ Jesus took hold of me. Brothers, I do not consider myself yet to have taken hold of it. But one thing I do: Forgetting what is behind and straining toward what is ahead, I press on toward the goal to win the prize for which God has called me heavenward in Christ Jesus. (Philippians 3:12-14)

If the apostle Paul, who was probably in his sixties, felt the need to continue to grow, how much more do you and I? The great pastor Philip Brooks said, "Character cannot be developed except by a steady, long, continued process." It has been observed that developing as a leader is a lot like investing in the stock market. If you hope to make a fortune in a day, you are not going to be very successful. Effective leaders know that personal growth is an ongoing process. The goal each day is to get a little better, to build on the previous day's progress.

Personal growth should be occurring in four key areas of life

The early years of Jesus' life are summarized in this simple statement,

And Jesus grew in wisdom and stature, and in favor with God and men. (Luke 2:52)

Note that Jesus grew in four key areas:
  1.) *Wisdom:* When was the last time you deliberately fed your mind? When seated, read a book; when moving, listen to a tape.
  2.) *Stature:* Physical health is the result of proper diet, rest, and exercise.
  3.) *Favor with God:* Spiritual growth increases through such important spiritual disciplines as personal Bible reading and study, prayer, and fasting.
  4.) *Favor with man:* We must continually invest in the key relationships of our lives to grow socially.

If Jesus needed to grow in these four areas, how much more must you and I?

Personal growth is the product of daily habits

The secret to effectiveness is found in our daily habits. Effective people and leaders build necessary disciplines into their lives and live those disciplines daily. Personal fitness is like physical fitness. It comes from learning the right exercises and doing them regularly until they become habits.

My Testimony of the Power of Personal Growth:

I have been told that I am an unusually disciplined person. However, several years ago I began to feel the need to increase all of my levels of personal effectiveness. This included leadership effectiveness, physical health, spiritual capacity, and the quality of my relationship with my wife and sons. I made the choice to aggressively invest time in a more disciplined and challenging personal growth plan that addressed the areas in which I needed to grow.

I made it a goal to build several disciplines into my schedule. Daily, I would hug my sons and tell them I loved them. I wanted to do something special, one-on-one with each of my three boys each week. We tried to have family devotions three to four nights a week. Daily, I would try to either serve or really listen to my wife. I tried to listen to two teaching cassette tapes a week and read one book a week or so. I tried to have one 30-minute personal prayer time daily and fast one day a week. I read my Bible almost daily. I attempted to exercise a half an hour, five days a week. I severely limited the time I spent watching TV.

Often, I did not quite reach all my goals, but by the end of a few months, I could tell the difference. I was making progress in all the key areas of my life. When one area would seem like it needed to be addressed I would hit it harder the next month.

Over the past few years of being aggressive with my growth plan, I have slowly made strides in all the key areas of my life. I have read hundreds of books and listened to hundreds of hours of Bible teaching or leadership training on tape. I have read through the Bible several times. I see answered prayer almost everyday. I have good relationships with my wife and sons. I now exercise about 40 minutes daily.

Every part of my life is better, including my ministry. My church has doubled in attendance. People tell me the anointing on my speaking and leading has noticeably increased. I have seen God multiply my small group numerous times. I am enjoying life more than ever.

If you are serious about reaching your potential, you need to have an aggressive growth plan. It might not be as aggressive as mine, but make sure it is challenging for you. Effectiveness in such a plan is the result of following "The Ten Commandments of Personal Growth."

The Ten Commandments of Personal Growth

1. Make the choice to be an ever-growing person.

Who you are today is the result of the choices you have made in the past. Who you will be tomorrow will be the result of the choices you make today. You will not significantly grow until you choose to do what it takes to grow. It starts with your choice. Your abilities are a gift from God; what you do with those abilities is your gift to God. Give God your best. Choose to do your part to grow and be the best you can be.

2. Focus your activities and set some goals.

Some effective small group leaders have as many as one dozen daily/weekly goals, but that is too many if this is new to you. Start with a few that you can reach and build from there. Set some smart goals in a few key areas. SMART goals are:

- *Simple.* A good simple goal is to read your Bible 15 minutes, or two chapters, a day. Two chapters a day will get you through the Bible twice every three years.
- *Measurable.* A measurable goal is tied to time (15 minutes a day) or to accomplishment (a chapter a day). It is something you can easily tell whether or not you hit.
- *Attainable.* You may have a simple, measurable goal that does you no good because it is too far beyond your reach. If you have never exercised in your life, starting at an hour a day would not be attainable. But starting with ten minutes a day would be reasonable.

- *Relevant.* Select goals that connect with your needs. For example, for a period in my life, I needed to make it a goal to hug my kids and tell them I love them daily. But maybe you already do that or don't have any kids.

   Maybe you need to get in better physical shape in order to be more spiritually effective. So set a goal to meet that need. But maybe you are an aerobics instructor and exercise is not an area that you need addressed. Pick goals that address the areas in which you need to grow.

- *Time-oriented.* If your goal is to read through the Bible but you have no time tied to it, you probably will never get it done. But if you have a goal to read through the Bible in a year, it will motivate and stretch you to read the three or more chapters a day needed to get through the Bible in a year.

3. Gather any needed tools.

There may be some tools you need to get the maximum benefit from your growth plan. For me, the key tool is my notebook/journal that has my growth plan chart written into the back pages. I check things off every morning as I read my Bible, pray, journal, and exercise. Then, I check off the reading, tapes, and family relationship investments from the previous day.

Other tools may be a good Bible, a prayer notebook, exercise clothes and equipment, books, or good teachings on cassette tape. I highly recommend that any small group leader read at least one good book on small group ministry each year. (Cell Group Resources™, a part of TOUCH® Outreach Ministries, has a comprehensive list of excellent resources.)

Realize that the small amount of money you invest in these tools is an investment in your personal growth. As you look back on your growth, the investment will be minimal compared to the benefits you will reap.

4. Develop a plan that fits you.

Jim works long hours and is a committed husband and father. He is also an effective small group leader who multiplies his group annually. He found that he was having a difficult time getting into the Word on his own. So he analyzed his schedule and found that he was spending about an hour a day commuting to work. He got the Bible on cassette and now spends about an hour a day listening to the Word on his way to and from work.

Those who are effective in personal growth do not adopt other peoples' plans. They prayerfully develop plans that fit them. Then, they adjust their plans with new goals and disciplines each month.

As you grow, your goals will grow. As you develop, you will find new areas to add to your plan. As strengths are gained, certain areas will no longer need to be a part of your plan. As your life changes, so must your plan.

5. Schedule the needed time

It was Henry Ford who said, "It is my observation that most successful people get ahead in the time other people waste." Growth takes time. Make appointments with yourself to work on your growth plan. You might find that you need to get up earlier. Or you may discover that in order to have the time to grow, you will have little or no time to watch TV. Most of us have, and waste, all the time we need to live out a good growth plan.

I suggest that you try to find an hour a day to work on personal growth. This time can include Bible reading, prayer, book reading, and exercise. It can be broken into increments of 10-30 minutes. You may do some of it in the morning and some in the evening.

6. Sow before you hope to reap.

Paul gave us an awesome spiritual principle when he said, "Do not be deceived: God cannot be mocked. A man reaps what he sows" (Galatians 6:7). Farmers will tell you that the law of sowing and reaping cannot be avoided or cheated. The law of the harvest has several unavoidable realities:

- You have to sow in order to reap. If no seed is sown, no harvest will be reaped.
- You have to sow the right things in order to reap the right things. You can't sow weeds and hope to reap corn.
- You have to sow before you reap. You can't cram for harvest. You need to plant in the spring, or you will never reap in the fall. Cutting corners and waiting till the last minute just won't work.

Those who are effective in personal growth live a life of sowing the positive things in order to enjoy a positive harvest. They work hard now in order to enjoy the results later. Look at the time you spend on personal growth as seeds sown that will one day begin to yield a great multiplying harvest.

Those who are effective in personal growth know that you have to pay now if you want to play later. Of course, if you play now, you will pay later. And it will be much more costly. Pay the price to grow daily, and you will soon begin to see the results of your effort.

The advent of day trading on the stock market has been a modern-day wake up call to many who have wanted to by-pass the law of the harvest. For the tiny handful fortunate enough to make some money in a brief time, thousands have lost great sums of money by trying for a quick harvest. Those who know warn that the way to make money in the stock market is through regular investments and long term patience.

Learn to look at the time you spend in personal growth as an investment in your personal portfolio and net worth. See the Lord multiplying your investments, and one day, giving you great spiritual riches as the reward.

Earl Nightingale stated, "If anyone will spend one hour a day on the same subject that person will be an expert on that subject." Nightingale is right. Since reading this quote several years ago, I have made it my practice to pick a subject and try to invest a hour daily on it for a year. I like to "master" it to the point of writing a book or seminar on the subject. For example, several years ago I started learning more about leadership. At the end of that year, I wrote what I had learned into a seminar and got to travel around lecturing church leaders on leadership. Over the past several years, I have developed a level of 'expertise' on such subjects as team ministry, prayer and fasting, revival, church health and growth, spiritual warfare, parenting, and small groups. On each subject I have developed a book or seminar in order to bless others with what I have learned. This all grew out of reading an hour a day on that subject, and the discipline came from my personal growth plan.

7. Make yourself accountable.

There are many papers I wrote in school that I never would have written without the accountability of a teacher and a grade. Many of us do better when we know that there is someone watching our progress. This is human nature.

So use the power of accountability to your advantage by making yourself accountable for your personal growth plan. Ask your small group coach to hold you accountable for your progress. Keep a chart of your progress. Write it into the goals you turn in to your small group pastor.

8. Share what you learn with others.

Dr. Elmer Towns is an amazing man. He is 67 years old and going strong. He is continually growing and continually being used by God. He lives by a simple principle: he learns to teach and teaches to learn.

Everything he learns he teaches. What he learns becomes a lesson, a class, a book, a resource packet, or a seminar. It may become a lesson that he will teach at his church. It may become a course for his college or seminary students — he is the dean of Liberty University School of Religion. It may become a new book — he publishes three a year. Or it could become a new seminar — he has given seminars all over America and around the world. Or it might end up as a resource packet — one such packet, *Friend Day*, is the best selling such item in history.

You will only remember about five percent of what you hear or read. But if you share what you heard or read with someone else, you will remember a much higher percentage. Take a minute each day to pass on what God is teaching you. Tell your spouse. Teach your kids. Share it with your group.

9. Associate with growing people.

The book of Proverbs tells us, "As iron sharpens iron, so one man sharpens another." (Proverbs 27:17). Growing people associate with growing people. They get and stay sharp, by being in the presence of sharp people.

Some call this the hot poker principle. In a fire, a poker gets hot just by being near the fire. In life, spiritual heat comes from spiritually hot people. In order to get spiritually hot, one needs to be close to spiritually hot people. There are two ways to do this: personally and vicariously. Personally, we get close to growing people by spending time with them, talking with them, and listening to them. Several years ago, I made it a goal to befriend all the pastors in my area who had churches larger than mine. I invited them to lunch. I picked their brains and tried to learn something significant each time I spent time with them. Now, I eat with some of them regularly. I have grown by my association with them. Vicariously, I have also grown by reading the books and listening to the tapes of other growing people. I do not know them personally, but I have grown by my relationship with them. I have applied their principles to my own life.

10. Put what you learn into practice.

The old saying goes, "Use it or lose it." The goal of personal growth is not to fill your head with information but to change your life. Try to put everything you are learning into practice. Try it. Live it. Do it.

When I read a book, I like to summarize each chapter into two sentences, one sentence to remember and one to do. This way, I take it into my life long after the book is finished.

In this book, there are charts to fill out at the end of each chapter in order to help you apply what you are learning. If you haven't done so already, go back and fill them in. And after you have filled them in, do what you have written.

The rest of this chapter is the opportunity for you to put what you have been learning into practice.

Sample Growth Goals

Grow mentally by:
- Reading a _____ a _____
- Listening to _____ tape(s) a _____

Develop spiritual fitness by:
- Reading the Bible _____ minutes daily or _____chapters daily.
- Praying _____ minutes daily.
- Journaling _____ minutes daily.
- Leading family devotions _____ minutes a day,
  _____ days a week.
- Fasting _____ days a month.

Increasing physical fitness by:
- Exercising _____ minutes _____ days a week.
- Sleeping _____ hours a night.
- Eating less _____ and more _____

Investing in relationships with:
- Spouse _____ minutes a day/hours a week.
- Children _____ minutes a day/hours a week.
- Apprentice _____ minutes a day/hours a week.
- Other _____ minutes a day/hours a week.

Sample Personal Growth Plan

Day	Mental		Spiritual		Physical	Social	
	Book	Tape	Prayer	Bible	Exercise	Family Devotion	Spouse
Monday							
Tuesday							
Wednesday							
Thursday							
Friday							
Saturday							
Sunday							

Putting It All Together

As I have taught the eight habits of effective small group leaders, the response is usually the same. People are excited and ready to go. But they look at it and ask, "How will I find the time to do all of this?"

Inspiration and information without application leads to frustration. This may be the most important chapter in this book because it helps you apply what you have learned to your life. You have learned the eight habits of a highly effective small group leader. Now that you know the habits and how to do them, the challenge is putting it all together. How can you apply all you have learned? How will you find the time to become a highly effective small group leader?

The key to applying the eight habits is planning them into your daily schedule. You need to have a time when you will work on each habit. I have found that the leaders who plan them into their schedules do them successfully. And those who don't plan them into their schedules don't do them at all.

There are three tools that will help you plan these habits into your life. They are the weekly goal sheet, the ideal week worksheet, and the actual week worksheet. The weekly goal sheet is a place to set a goal for how much time you will spend on

> *The highly effective small group leader plans the eight habits into his or her schedule.*

each habit every week. The ideal week worksheet is a schedule for when you hope to spend time working on each habit. The actual week worksheet is a record of when you actually spent time working on those habits.

The challenge is balancing the ideal with the real and investing time regularly into each habit. As a leader, I rarely have a week where I reach the ideal. By knowing the habits and spending some time on each of them regularly, I still make progress and see my group grow and multiply.

Let me remind you that we are talking about eight "habits." A habit is "a thing done often and hence done easily. It is a practice or act that is acquired and has become automatic."[1] Therefore, let me encourage you to use these tools for a couple of months. It requires three weeks to develop a new habit and six weeks of use until it feels comfortable. So you will need to use these worksheets for at least the first six weeks as you develop your habits. You may need to go back and use them periodically to keep you in balance and on track with all eight habits.

Weekly Goal Sheet

Listing the amount of time you want to spend developing each habit in a given week is very valuable. Some of the habits are daily disciplines like prayer and personal growth. Others are weekly practices, like contacting, mentoring, or inviting new people. Set a goal for the amount of time you will try to give to each habit for that particular week.

Weekly Goal Sheet *(Sample)*

	DAILY	WEEKLY
Dream	5 minutes	.5 hours or 30 minutes
Pray	30 minutes	2.5 hours or 150 minutes
Invite		.5 hours or 30 minutes
Contact		1.5 hours or 90 minutes
Mentor		1 hour or 60 minutes
Prepare		1.5 hours or 90 minutes
Grow	30 minutes	3.5 hours or 210 minutes
Fellowship		1 hour or 60 minutes
TOTAL		12 hours

Comments on Using the Weekly Goal Sheet

- The sample shows a fairly ambitious set of goals that would require 12 hours a week. This may sound overwhelming. It might seem less overwhelming when you realize that prayer and personal growth are things you are already doing but haven't seen as habits of a highly effective small group leader before.
- A tithe of our waking hours is about 11-12 hours a week. Therefore, if a leader would give a tithe of his time, he would be able to invest significantly into all eight habits every week. Everyone I have known who invests this amount of time into these eight habits grows and multiplies their groups.
- If you cannot spend 11-12 hours a week working outside the group, don't be discouraged. See it as a goal to work toward. The habits will work as long as you invest time in them regularly. The more time you invest, the more rapidly your group will grow and multiply.
- Dreaming is probably something you won't really need to schedule. It probably will not require any extra time. You can do it while you do other things like showering, driving, or praying.
- Fellowship and inviting are other areas you may not invest in weekly, but you will need to invest in them regularly. One two-hour fellowship activity a month averages out to half an hour a week.   Setting up the activity can come from time you spend contacting people.

Ideal Week Worksheet

Leaders who take a few minutes each week to plan the eight habits into their schedules are much more likely to apply them. The ideal week worksheet is a place to tentatively schedule the eight habits into your week. It is called ideal because things won't always go according to plan or right on schedule. The best approach is to set specific times for certain habits. Make a weekly appointment with yourself to prepare, mentor, contact, and invite. Make daily appointments to pray and work on personal growth areas. Make weekly or monthly appointments for fellowship.

Ideal Week Worksheet (Sample)

	Monday	Tuesday	Wednesday	Thursday	Friday	Saturday	Sunday	TOTAL
Dream	Last 5 minutes before going to sleep	Last 5 minutes before going to sleep	Last 5 minutes before going to sleep	Last 5 minutes before going to sleep	Last 5 minutes before going to sleep	Last 5 minutes before going to sleep		30 minutes
Pray	6:00-6:30 AM	6:00-6:30 AM	6:00-6:30 AM	6:00-6:30 AM	6:00-6:30 AM	6:00-6:30 AM	6:00-6:30 AM	3.5 hours
Invite	7:00-7:30 PM Phone calls							30 minutes
Contact		7:00-8:00 PM Phone calls	6:30-7:00 PM Before group					1 hour
Mentor								30 minutes
Prepare	7:30-8:30 PM	8:00-8:30 PM						1.5 hours
Grow	6:30-7:15 AM Bible and book 8:30-9:00 PM exercise	6:30-7:15 AM Bible and book 8:30-9:00 PM exercise	6:30-7:15 AM Bible and book	6:30-7:15 AM Bible and book 8:30-9:00 PM exercise				4.5 hours
Fellowship					6:00-7:30 PM dinner with group members			1.5 hours

Comments on Using the Ideal Week Worksheet

• The key to applying the eight habits is matching the ideal with the real. Scheduling helps make the ideal real. Try to find a time to accomplish your goals.

• You may find that your goals were not attainable. If so, modify them to fit the time available.

• Write these times on your calendar or into your appointment book. Try to keep them as you would any other appointment you make.

Actual Week Worksheet

The actual week worksheet is a place to record the progress you actually make on the eight habits each week. It is where you write down the time you spent on each of the habits that week. It is best to fill it out as you go or at the end of the day, instead of trying to remember it all at the end of the week.

Actual Week Worksheet (Sample)

	Monday	Tuesday	Wednesday	Thursday	Friday	Saturday	Sunday	TOTAL
Dream	5 minutes	5 minutes	5 minutes	5 minutes	5 minutes			25 minutes
Pray	6:00-6:30 AM	6:00-6:30 AM		6:00-6:15 AM		6:00-7:00 AM	6:00-6:30 AM	2.75 hours
Invite	7:00-8:00 PM Phone calls							1 hour
Contact		7:00-7:45 PM Phone calls						45 minutes
Mentor			Missed mentor time			7:00-8:00 AM Coffee meeting		1 hour
Prepare		8:00-9:00 PM				7:30-8:00 PM		1.5 hours
Grow	6:30-7:00 AM Bible	6:30-7:00 AM Bible	6:30-7:00 AM Bible	6:30-7:00 AM Bible 7:00-8:00 PM exercise	6:30-7:00 AM Bible	7:00-8:00 PM book		4.5 hours
Fellowship				7:00-9:00 PM Group BBQ at park				2 hours

Comments on Using the Actual Week Worksheet

- Filling out the Actual Week Worksheet at the end of each day only takes a few moments, but these moments are very valuable.
- Filling out this sheet serves as an excellent means of personal accountability. I try to do well on keeping my goals because I love checking off the completed appointments.
- These sheets become a lasting basis of evaluation. For example, it is possible to look back after a few weeks and see that the reason your group's attendance is up is because you have spent more time contacting or inviting.
- A completed sheet provides a wonderful source of encouragement. You can feel great knowing that you are sowing good seed that will eventually, if not immediately, lead to a good harvest.

Your Turn

Now that you know the habits and have the tools, take the time to set your own goals and schedule your own week. If this is all new to you, start small and build week by week. Maybe you have your own plan. That is great. The best plan is a plan you know you will use. Any plan will work as long as it has all eight habits built into your week often enough to become true habits and to make a difference. Take the time to fill out these sheets. As you begin to live the eight habits, you are on your way to becoming a highly effective small group leader.

Weekly Goal Sheet

	DAILY	WEEKLY
Dream		
Pray		
Invite		
Contact		
Mentor		
Prepare		
Grow		
Fellowship		
TOTAL		

Ideal Week Worksheet

	Monday	Tuesday	Wednesday	Thursday	Friday	Saturday	Sunday	TOTAL
Dream								
Pray								
Invite								
Contact								
Mentor								
Prepare								
Grow								
Fellowship								

Actual Week Worksheet

	Monday	Tuesday	Wednesday	Thursday	Friday	Saturday	Sunday	TOTAL
Dream								
Pray								
Invite								
Contact								
Mentor								
Prepare								
Grow								
Fellowship								

THE EIGHT HABITS OF
EFFECTIVE CHURCHES

Part Two

The Eight Habits
for Leaders of Leaders

Steve and Rod were members of the first small group I led at our church. Soon, they were leading their own groups. As their groups multiplied, they began to coach other small group leaders. Today, both of them are pastors at our church. Steve is the Discipleship/Assimilation Pastor and Rod is the Membership/Small Groups Pastor. As they lead leaders, they continue to use the habits they learned as small group leaders.

The single greatest tool in the leader's hand is example. If you want your small group leaders living the eight habits, then small group leader coaches and other leaders of leaders must also be living the eight habits. Without exception, those leaders who live the eight habits will have a higher percentage of leaders under them living the habits than those who don't.

Once you have had the joy of multiplying your group several times, you may find yourself leading the leaders of those groups in place of or along with your group. These leaders are people you mentored to lead a group, and now that they are leading groups of their own, the mentoring should not end. Group leaders need ongoing encouragement and ministry just as much as group members do.

Different churches structure their leadership differently. Many have levels with spans of care covering five to ten leaders. For example, in our church, we like to have a coach for every five or six group leaders. We have found that leaders without coaches tend not to multiply and often get discouraged or burn out. We try not to have lay coaches overseeing more than six group leaders. We also like to have a director for every six coaches and a pastor over every six directors. Some churches call these people supervisors and section leaders, district leaders, or pastors and zone pastors.

Small Group Ministry *(Sample)*

LEVEL OF LEADERSHIP	TITLE OF LEADER	SPAN OF OVERSIGHT
ONE	Small Group Leader	10 Group Members
TWO	Coach	Up to 6 Small Group Leaders
THREE	Director	Up to 6 Coaches
FOUR	Small Group Pastor	Up to 6 Directors

The beauty of the eight habits is that they are applicable at all levels of small group oversight. We try to get apprentices starting to live them. We expect our leaders to live them. We require our coaches to practice them with their leaders. Once someone learns the habits as an apprentice, she can continue to use the habits as she progresses up the levels of leadership. The eight habits transfer easily from one level to another.

Applying the Eight Habits to Leaders of Leaders

1. Dream.

The effective coach dreams about and sets goals for the health of the groups, the number of groups, and the multiplication of the group leaders. The habit of dreaming must extend up the ladder of ministry to the directors and pastors.

Currently, Rod, our Small Group Pastor, oversees about 100 groups. But he dreams of this growing to 200 groups in the next five years. Matt, our Student Ministry Director, dreams of multiplying his groups from 20 to 40. Joyce, our Women's Groups coach, has the dream of seeing her 12 groups grow to 25.

2. Pray.

Just as effective group leaders grow their groups on their knees, so do effective coaches in growing their groups. They spend time each day praying for the spiritual health of their groups and group leaders. They pray for the new apprentices that their leaders are recruiting. They pray for the multiplication of their groups. They pray for their coaching apprentices.

In the same way, effective directors pray for their group coaches. They pray for the spiritual health of those under their authority. They pray for the apprentices who are on the way to leadership. They pray for the mentoring abilities of their leaders. They pray for the people they are mentoring as coaches or future directors. Pastors do the same for their directors.

3. Invite.

Effective small group coaches don't just focus on their current leaders. They have a heart for those who are not yet leaders and coaches. Effective coaches must set the pace by inviting new leaders to pursue apprenticeship. As they visit groups, they are on the lookout for new leaders. They help the leaders under their authority discover potential leaders and recruit them to apprenticeship as future small group leaders. They help the leaders under them develop their apprentices into effective leaders who apply the eight habits to their lives.

In similar fashion, directors are on the look out for potential coaches. They help their coaches find people to mentor, and then help mentor them.

4. Contact.

Effective coaches make sure that their small group leaders are contacted frequently, consistently, and effectively. Effective directors contact their coaches, and effective pastors contact their directors. They put in the time necessary to build strong relationships.

Just as group membership and attendance improve when members are contacted, group leaders' attendance of coaching sessions improves when they are contacted. Just as group members stay focused on outreach and growth when they are contacted, so do group leaders. Just as group members feel loved and important because they are contacted, so do group leaders.

The key to any effective small group system is the ongoing care of the people within that system. When they do not feel cared for they lose interest. This is just as true of group leaders, coaches, and directors as it is of group members. They all need to be contacted.

It does not matter how leaders are contacted. What matters is that they are contacted. Most of our coaches like to use the phone to do contacting. They call every leader every week. Others especially enjoy "church chats," which are fifteen minute, touch-base conversations in between services every Sunday morning.

5. Prepare.

Effective coaches prepare for their meetings with their leaders. Directors prepare for their meetings with their coaches, and pastors prepare with their meetings with their directors. These meetings should occur both as a group of leaders and one on one with the coach/director/pastor. One of our directors likes to meet his coaches for breakfast regularly. Another one meets her leaders in a bakery/coffee shop. Another one prefers the one-on-one meetings. Choose the method that best suits your needs, but try to use at least some of each variety.

In these meetings a coach may prepare several things.

- After a coach visits a group, she should share feedback and tips with the leader of that group regarding the group meeting. Each of the elements of the meeting should be discussed. Always try to give feedback that is more positive then negative.
- A coach asks her leader(s) how they are doing on each of the eight habits. The coach may ask to see each leader's weekly goals, ideal week, and actual week worksheets.
- A coach asks each leader about progress on their personal growth plan.
- A coach gives every leader additional training on the eight habits for outside of the group or enhancing the elements of the actual group meeting.
- A coach keeps each leader informed about upcoming church and group events.
- A coach discusses apprentices with each leader.
- A coach discusses multiplication dates for each leader's group.
- A coach gives advice regarding practical things like space concerns, child-care issues, and scheduling conflicts.
- A coach prays with each of her leaders.

Effective directors and pastors can apply the same meeting elements when meeting with the leaders under them. Leaders must invest time preparing to share with those under them. Their time is precious and so is yours. Don't waste it by being unprepared. Make these times as encouraging and as valuable as possible.

6. Mentor.

Mentoring provides two major benefits. First, it creates multiplication. A coach needs to be mentoring future coaches in order to multiply the coaching ministry. Directors need to mentor future directors and pastors need to mentor future pastors. Successful leaders are constantly multiplying themselves by developing successors.

Second, mentoring prepares the church for greater harvest. If a church has a strong mentoring process, the church will avoid trouble if God sends a growth boom. It will be able to capture and go with the growth that God sends.

One of my friends is the senior pastor of a large church made up of many small groups. Several years ago, their groups began to explode. Everything looked wonderful as people were being saved and groups were bursting at the seams. New groups were being birthed weekly. Yet the mentoring process was not well developed, and people were stepping into leadership unprepared. As the unprepared stepped into leadership, the wheels came off. Leaders burnt out. People got hurt. Conflicts arose. It took them nearly ten years to regain their numbers and momentum.

7. Grow.

Growing coaches will lead growing leaders. Growing directors will lead growing coaches, and growing pastors will lead growing directors. Personal growth is very important for the leaders of leaders. They need to continually learn, grow, and improve. They need to have growth plans that match, if not surpass, those of the leaders under them.

Every coach, director, and pastor needs to set the example for those under them by following challenging growth plans and sharing them with those under them. They need to set a growth climate and a leadership atmosphere. They need to pass on helpful articles, books, and tapes to the leaders under them.

The way I got the leaders under me to adopt a growth plan followed these steps, which you can adopt or modify to fit your needs.
- I whet their appetites by sharing challenging information from books I was reading and quotes from tapes I was listening to.
- I asked them what they were reading or listening to that had especially challenged them in the past weeks.
- I taught the "what, why, and how" of a personal growth plan in group meetings.
- I asked them to set up a simple growth plan for a short time.
- I periodically checked up on their progress.

8. Fellowship.

Effective leaders of leaders use the power of fellowship to build up those they oversee. Leaders may not need fellowship as often, but they need it just a much. They especially need times where they don't have to be the ministers or the leaders, where they get ministered to and led. They need times to blow off steam and relax. Effective leaders of leaders will create times and opportunities for those under them to enjoy fellowship with one another.

Use the list given in chapter seven to formulate a plan that provides fellowship activities for those you lead.

9. Putting It All Together.

Leaders of small group leaders are just like their small group leaders: well intentioned and very busy. Highly effective leaders of leaders use the tools, or develop their own, to put the eight habits in their own schedules. They set the pace for those under them by making wise and regular use of the weekly goal sheets, the ideal week worksheets, and the actual week worksheets. They should be doing as much or more than they expect of those under them. They should be models of personal discipline and effectiveness. They should live the eight habits as well or better than anyone coming along under them.

Leaders find it motivating when those placed in authority pull out their goal sheets or actual week worksheets. Take the time to fill out these worksheets for yourself, adopting the habits to your role as a leader of leaders. Share your progress with the leaders under you and the leader over you.

Weekly Goal Sheet

	DAILY	WEEKLY
Dream		
Pray		
Invite		
Contact		
Mentor		
Prepare		
Grow		
Fellowship		
TOTAL		

Ideal Week Worksheet

	Monday	Tuesday	Wednesday	Thursday	Friday	Saturday	Sunday	TOTAL
Dream								
Pray								
Invite								
Contact								
Mentor								
Prepare								
Grow								
Fellowship								

Actual Week Worksheet

	Monday	Tuesday	Wednesday	Thursday	Friday	Saturday	Sunday	TOTAL
Dream								
Pray								
Invite								
Contact								
Mentor								
Prepare								
Grow								
Fellowship								

Becoming an "Eight Habits" Church

For several years, our church wrestled with its focus. It became more of a church with small groups, instead of a church of small groups. Most of the groups we had lacked apprentices and coaches. They were not growing, and few multiplied. We realized that we needed to focus aggressively on the development of small group leaders and revamp our small group structure. In a period of a few years, we got back on track and were ministering at a higher level. Most of our current groups are healthy, growing, and multiplying. We now have over 100 groups and are seeing God raising up awesome leaders. Our church is becoming a powerful eight habits church.

Suggestions for Becoming an "Eight Habits" Church

1. Prepare for change.

The leaders of the church need to assess the impact this change will have on the church. How many people will it affect? How deeply will it affect them? Will becoming an eight habits church be a small tweak to your existing system, or will it be a complete overhaul?

For us to get where we wanted, we realized that we would need to disassemble our existing Sunday morning Adult Bible Congregation system. It was popular with many of those involved, but the system had ceased growing and was not producing leaders. They took up parking and classrooms that we needed on Sunday mornings. It took away from small groups. We needed to transition ministry away from Adult Bible Congregations and toward small groups.

Before we actually changed anything, I spent one night a week for seven months meeting with church families as part of my responsibilities as the Senior Pastor. I invited them to my home ten couples at a time and shared the vision of our church with them. I started with the initial vision for our church to be a multiplying church that would reach as many people as deeply as possible. I told the story of our beginnings. I shared a history of God's blessings and talked about our strengths and our future. Then I explained the "whats" and "whys" of our transition away from Adult Bible Congregations. I emphasized reaching the lost and multiplying small groups. I answered questions and listened to concerns. The personal meetings allowed me to sense who was resistant and to gain a better understanding of their concerns.

It took a great deal of time and effort to speak face to face with the families in our church. But this made our transition as painless as possible. I did not jump back into small group leadership and coaching until after this seven month period was complete. When I did, most of our people understood and supported the change.

We follow a simple rule of thumb: "The bigger the change, the longer the preparation time and the more persuasion will be needed." Many well-meaning pastors have ruined their ministry by managing change poorly. People will fight change unless they learn so much that they can envision it, or they hurt so much that they embrace it.

We must teach them. Lead them. Love them through the changes. We must give them time to work through the process.

Managing change works better when you already know the influencers in your church and work to influence them. They will influence many. You should also raise up new influencers who have bought into the new vision. They will influence many more.

2. The senior pastor must lead the charge.

The most effective influencer in most churches is the Senior Pastor. In order for us to get where we needed to be, I had to dedicate a few years of my life to being a champion of groups at our church. For me this took several forms:

- I led a small group. As a small group leader, I could model the eight habits of a highly effective small group leader for all of the other leaders. I had fresh illustrations about the importance and elements of group life.
- I coached small group leaders. As a coach, I could model the eight habits of an effective coach. I could keep abreast of the struggles leaders face.

- I assumed leadership of a district of groups. As a district leader, I could model the eight habits on this level and work to raise up highly effective coaches.
- I carved time out of my schedule to read books on small group ministry, attend small group seminars, and meet with our pastoral staff. We cobbled out a philosophy and structure that fit our church.
- I used the pulpit to promote small groups through the use of illustrations and applications.

3. Build on what is already there.

Every church has preexisting values and structures. Don't just throw these away or belittle them. This only hurts people's feelings and makes them resistant to change. It hurts your credibility if you were championing these programs a year ago and now make fun of them as you champion a new one. If your church has a history of evangelism, build on it. If the ethos is discipleship, build on that.

We had a structure of Adult Bible Congregations that needed to be transitioned. Where we incorporated the existing leaders into the vision, the transition went well. Where we failed to do this, the transition met resistance. A few people got upset and eventually left the church. We could have done a better job by building on the values and benefits people received from the Adult Bible Congregations.

4. Start where you are and use the eight habits to develop highly effective leaders, coaches, etc.

We wanted to get the eight habits into the DNA of our church leaders. So we went back and re-trained existing leaders. Most bought into the new vision, though some did not.

Don't fight those who don't immediately jump on the change bandwagon. Simply love them, and make what is going on with the change so exciting that they will want to participate in it.

We also tried to get all the new leaders and coaches living the eight habits. Those living the eight habits began to grow and multiply their groups. We recognized and rewarded this. Those who were slower to adopt change took note and began to come around.

5. Cast the vision.

A recent survey of churches and pastors revealed a powerful reality: Ninety percent of the pastors surveyed stated that the church existed for others, to evangelize the world, but 90 percent of the church members surveyed stated that the church existed to meet their needs.

People need to be reminded constantly of the vision for evangelism and discipling of the world. We often speak of the 850,000 unchurched people in our area. We talk about the 200,000 within driving distance of our church building.

Use all the available means to keep the vision in front of the people. Church members should keep hearing it from the pulpit, seeing it in the newsletter, observing it in the testimonies, and hearing it in the prayers.

The Nehemiah principle of vision casting is that the people need to be reminded every 30 days or they will get distracted and lose focus. Plan for the people to receive some type of reminder every three to four weeks.

6. Recognize, reward, and require.

Help leaders develop the habits by being committed to recognizing, rewarding, and requiring them as much as possible. Recognize eight habits leaders in sectional, district, and zone meetings. Recognize them in sermon illustrations. Recognize them in newsletter articles. Get them up front to pray. I have made a commitment not to mention a group unless I know the leader is trying to live the eight habits.

Reward eight habits leaders:
- Give them certificates and books in district and zone meetings.
- Spend more time with them.
- Buy them lunch.
- Brag on them publicly.
- Send them cards of appreciation.
- Only promote small group leaders who are eight habits leaders to the position of coach.

Require new leaders to be eight habits leaders. Have them sign a covenant each year. Require coaches, directors, and staff members to be eight habits people.

7. Promote.

Use the various avenues available to promote group life. We build our small group ministry around three seasons a year: Fall, September - December; Winter, January - April; and Summer, May - August. At the beginning of each season, we like to do several things to promote small groups. These include:
- Holding a Small Group Leaders Rally. We feed our leaders, minister to them, challenge them, recognize them, reward them, and send them out for a new season of ministry. Last fall it had a football theme and felt like a pep rally.
- Having a Small Group Sunday. We especially use these in fall and winter to promote groups, recast the vision, recognize and commission new

leaders, and recruit new people into groups. Some components include:

    1.) A sermon about the value of group life.

    2.) A special drama about the value of groups.

    3.) Testimonies from group members and leaders

    4.) A commissioning prayer for new leaders.

    5.) Recognition of multiplying groups and new leaders.

    6.) Organizing leaders in matching "group leader" golf-shirts.

    7.) Tables in the foyer where people can sign up for groups.

    8.) A new catalogue of group offerings for that season.

- Having a regular place in your bulletin or newsletter for info on small groups. Recognize new groups and have testimonies of how groups met a need or changed a person's life.
- Discussing the importance of small groups with every new member. We have our Groups Pastor teach a lesson in our New Members class on the value of small group involvement. We require new members to get involved in a group as a part of their membership commitment.
- Having a wall in the church lobby, with contact cards available describing each group.
- Having a connection center near or in front of the wall with a desk or kiosk and person available to answer questions and sign people up for groups.
- Having banners with group goals prominently displayed in the church.
- Giving the leaders laminated cards with the eight habits listed on them.
- Giving t-shirts and hats to leaders, acknowledging the number of years they have been eight habits leaders.
- Highlighting an eight habits leader and his or her group in the bulletin every week.

8. Model.

Nothing speaks more loudly than example. Changing the behaviors of others begins when we show them what the expected behavior looks like. Authority and credibility flow from example. Until you are willing to live the eight habits, you cannot expect anyone else to.

As a Senior Pastor, I could not continue leading a couple of groups, coaching a dozen leaders, and leading a district of 25 groups. So I trained and mentored others to fill some of these roles and take them to a new level.

I will probably always continue to lead at least one group. I like being on the front lines and being able to speak to leaders with insight fresh from the trenches. I like seeing how group life changes people's lives. I like growing a group, incorporating new people, and raising up new leaders. I must constantly set the example. As a group leader, I need to practice the eight habits. But they do not become a burden, because I know they work, and I need to be effective in order to fulfill God's calling on my life.

9. Pray.

Prayer is not mentioned last because it is least important but to make it stick in your mind. The importance of prayer *cannot* be underestimated. Nothing of eternal significance ever happens apart from prayer. Everything good is born and bred in prayer. Prayer is not the only work, but it is the work that makes all of our other work effective. Pray about becoming an eight habits church. Pray through each step of the process.

Prayer brings God into each situation. Bathe your transition in prayer. As a result of prayer, God will show you how He wants you to go about becoming an eight habits church. God will overcome obstacles, change people's hearts, and help people see the vision. God will make all the difference.

Putting it to Work

- Which of these nine suggestions for becoming an eight habits church do you need to apply?

- Which one should you begin with?

- What specific steps should you take as soon as possible?

EXTRA WORKSHEETS

Weekly Goal Sheet

	DAILY	WEEKLY
Dream		
Pray		
Invite		
Contact		
Mentor		
Prepare		
Grow		
Fellowship		
TOTAL		

Ideal Week Worksheet

	Monday	Tuesday	Wednesday	Thursday	Friday	Saturday	Sunday	TOTAL
Dream								
Pray								
Invite								
Contact								
Mentor								
Prepare								
Grow								
Fellowship								

Actual Week Worksheet

	Monday	Tuesday	Wednesday	Thursday	Friday	Saturday	Sunday	TOTAL
Dream								
Pray								
Invite								
Contact								
Mentor								
Prepare								
Grow								
Fellowship								

Sample Growth Goals

Grow mentally by:

- Reading a _____ a _____
- Listening to _____ tape(s) a _____

Develop spiritual fitness by:

- Reading the Bible _____ minutes daily or _____chapters daily.
- Praying _____ minutes daily.
- Journaling _____ minutes daily.
- Leading family devotions _____ minutes a day,

  _____ days a week.
- Fasting _____ days a month.

Increasing physical fitness by:

- Exercising _____ minutes _____ days a week.
- Sleeping _____ hours a night.
- Eating less _____ and more _____

Investing in relationships with:

- Spouse _____ minutes a day / hours a week.
- Children _____ minutes a day / hours a week.
- Apprentice _____ minutes a day / hours a week.
- Other _____ minutes a day / hours a week.

Sample Personal Growth Plan

	Mental		Spiritual		Physical	Social	
Day	**Book**	**Tape**	**Prayer**	**Bible**	**Exercise**	**Family Devotion**	**Spouse**
Monday							
Tuesday							
Wednesday							
Thursday							
Friday							
Saturday							
Sunday							

END NOTES:

Chapter 1:
[1] Joel Comiskey, *Home Group Cell Explosion* (Houston, TX: TOUCH® Publications, 1999), 47.

Chapter 2:
[1] Joel Comiskey, *Home Group Cell Explosion*, 34.

Chapter 3:
[1] Price and Springer, *Rapha's Handbook for Group Leaders* (Houston, TX: Rapha Publishing, 1991), 132.
[2] McIntosh and Martin, *Finding Them, Keeping Them* (Nashville, TN: Broadman Press 1992), 75.

Chapter 6:
[1] Joel Comiskey, *Leadership Explosion* (Houston, TX: TOUCH® Publications, 2001), 34.
[2] Bill Hull, *Jesus Christ Disciple Maker* (Old Tappan New Jersey: Fleming Revell), 119.
[3] Joel Comiskey, *Home Cell Group Explosion*, 46.

Chapter 9:
[1] *Webster's New World Dictionary of the American Language*, (New York, World Publishing), 649.

Additional Small Group Resources For Your Ministry

The Pocket Guide to Leading A Small Group
by Dave Earley and Rod Dempsey
This powerful little book has 52 ways to help you adopt the practices of a healthy small group leader. By reading a few pages each week and practicing what you learn, you'll be surprised at how you and your group will grow!

Turning Members Into Leaders
by Dave Earley
The best way to raise up new small group leaders is not to ask them to be leaders until they're fully trained. This excellent resource explains how to turn members into leaders who will say "Yes!" to leadership when you pop the question. If your small group ministry needs more leaders, this book is a must-read for all your leaders!

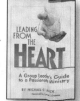

Leading From The Heart
by Michael Mack
Recharge your leaders and prevent burnout! Powerful small group leaders share a common trait: a passionate heart for God. They know their priorities and know that time with Him is always at the top of the list. This book will renew leaders' hearts, refocus their priorities and recharge their ministry.

How to be a Great Cell Group Coach
by Joel Comiskey
Research has proven that the greatest contributor to small group success is the quality of coaching provided for group leaders. This book provides a comprehensive guide for coaching small group group leaders.

The Pocket Guide to Coaching small groups
by Randall Neighbour
This short, pocket-sized book does an excellent job of illustrating the importance of friendship in the coaching role. It's easy to read and great for busy coaches. If they just won't read, hand them this booklet.

Community Life 101
by Randall Neighbour
When your church members join a group, do they really understand what being a part of a holistic small group requires? The author uses lighthearted and meaningful personal stories to drive home the fact that healthy small group life requires relationships outside of the weekly meeting and participation and transparency during meetings.